SADDAM HUSSEIN

صّدام حُسين

THE CHELSEA HOUSE LIBRARY OF BIOGRAPHY

SADDAM HUSSEIN

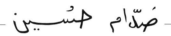

NITA M. RENFREW

Chelsea House Publishers

New York • Philadelphia

CHELSEA HOUSE PUBLISHERS

Editor-in-Chief   Richard S. Papale
Managing Editor   Karyn Gullen Browne
Copy Chief   Philip Koslow
Picture Editor   Adrian Allen
Art Director   Maria Epes
Assistant Art Director   Howard Brotman
Manufacturing Director   Gerald Levine
Production Coordinator   Marie Claire Cebrián

The Chelsea House Library of Biography

Staff for SADDAM HUSSEIN
Senior Editor   John W. Selfridge
Copy Editor   Christopher Duffy
Picture Researcher   Wendy P. Wills
Series Designer   Basia Niemczyc
Layout Artist   Robert Yaffe
Cover Illustration   Alan Nahigian

First Printing

1   3   5   7   9   8   6   4   2

Library of Congress Cataloging-in-Publication Data

Renfrew, Nita
Saddam Hussein/by Nita Renfrew.
p. cm.—(The Chelsea House library of biography)
Includes bibliographical references and index.
Describes the life of the Iraqi president, his rise to power, and his orchestration
of Iraqi troops during the Persian Gulf War.
ISBN 0-7910-1776-1
        0-7910-1775-3 (pbk.)
1. Hussein, Saddam, 1937– —Juvenile literature. 2. Presidents—Iraq—Biog-
raphy—Juvenile literature. [1. Hussein, Saddam, 1937– . 2. Presidents—Iraq.]
I. Title. II. Series.
DS79.66.H87R46 1992   91-33174
956.704'3'092—dc20   CIP
[B]   AC

Contents

THE CHELSEA HOUSE LIBRARY OF BIOGRAPHY

Other titles in the series are forthcoming.

Introduction

Learning from Biographies

Vito Perrone

The oldest narratives that exist are biographical. Much of what we know, for example, about the Pharaohs of ancient Egypt, the builders of Babylon, the philosophers of Greece, the rulers of Rome, the many biblical and religious leaders who provide the base for contemporary spiritual beliefs, has come to us through biographies—the stories of their lives. Although an oral tradition was long the mainstay of historically important biographical accounts, the oral stories making up this tradition became by the 1st century A.D. central elements of a growing written literature.

In the 1st century A.D., biography assumed a more formal quality through the work of such writers as Plutarch, who left us more than 500 biographies of political and intellectual leaders of Rome and Greece. This tradition of focusing on great personages lasted well into the 20th century and is seen as an important means of understanding the history of various times and places. We learn much, for example, from Plutarch's writing about the collapse of the Greek city-states and about the struggles in Rome over the justice and the constitutionality of a world empire. We also gain considerable understanding of the definitions of morality and civic virtue and how various common men and women lived out their daily existence.

Not surprisingly, the earliest American writing, beginning in the 17th century, was heavily biographical. Those Europeans who came to America were dedicated to recording their experience, especially the struggles they faced in building what they determined to be a new culture. John Norton's *Life and Death of John Cotton*, printed in 1630, typifies these early works. Later biographers often tackled more ambitious projects. Cotton Mather's *Magnalia Christi Americana*, published in 1702, accounted for the lives of more than 70 ministers and political leaders. In addition, a biographical literature around the theme of Indian captivity had considerable popularity. Soon after the American Revolution and the organization of the United States of America, Americans were treated to a large outpouring of biographies about such figures as Benjamin Franklin, George Washington, Thomas Jefferson, and Aaron Burr, among others. These particular works served to build a strong sense of national identity.

Among the diverse forms of historical literature, biographies have been over many centuries the most popular. And in recent years interest in biography has grown even greater, as biography has gone beyond prominent government figures, military leaders, giants of business, industry, literature, and the arts. Today we are treated increasingly to biographies of more common people who have inspired others by their particular acts of courage, by their positions on important social and political issues, or by their dedicated lives as teachers, town physicians, mothers, and fathers. Through this broader biographical literature, much of which is featured in the CHELSEA HOUSE LIBRARY OF BIOGRAPHY, our historical understandings can be enriched greatly.

What makes biography so compelling? Most important, biography is a human story. In this regard, it makes of history something personal, a narrative with which we can make an intimate connection. Biographers typically ask us as readers to accompany them on a journey through the life of another person, to see some part of the world through another's eyes. We can, as a result, come to understand what it is like to live the life of a slave, a farmer, a textile worker, an engineer, a poet, a president—in a sense, to walk in another's shoes. Such experience can be personally invaluable. We cannot ask for a better entry into historical studies.

Although our personal lives are likely not as full as those we are reading about, there will be in most biographical accounts many common experiences. As with the principal character of any biography, we are also faced with numerous decisions, large and small. In the midst of living our lives we are not usually able to comprehend easily the significance of our daily decisions or grasp easily their many possible consequences, but we can gain important insights into them by seeing the decisions made by others play themselves out. We can learn from others.

Because biography is a personal story, it is almost always full of surprises. So often, the personal lives of individuals we come across historically are out of view, their public personas masking who they are. It is through biography that we gain access to their private lives, to the acts that define who they are and what they truly care about. We see their struggles within the possibilities and limitations of life, gaining insight into their beliefs, the ways they survived hardships, what motivated them, and what discouraged them. In the process we can come to understand better our own struggles.

As you read this biography, try to place yourself within the subject's world. See the events as that person sees them. Try to understand why the individual made particular decisions and not others. Ask yourself if you would have chosen differently. What are the values or beliefs that guide the subject's actions? How are those values or beliefs similar to yours? How are they different from yours? Above all, remember: You are engaging in an important historical inquiry as you read a biography, but you are also reading a literature that raises important personal questions for you to consider.

Iraqi president Saddam Hussein attends a meeting in Baghdad on August 25, 1990. Earlier that month, Saddam ordered Iraqi troops to invade Kuwait in order to force a resolution to long-standing economic and territorial disputes between Iraq and Kuwait.

1

صّدّام حسَين

Kings

IT WAS LATE AFTERNOON ON AUGUST 1, 1990, and the Iraqi president, Saddam Hussein, was about to order his forces into Kuwait. His objective: to force a settlement of many long-standing issues that divided the two Arab countries.

In at least one way, August 1990 was like any other August in Baghdad, the Iraqi capital: It was oppressively hot. As the temperature soared, the air conditioners in Saddam's hardened bunker, deep below the Presidential Palace, worked overtime. Knowing that the intense heat of the day would work against his troops, Saddam waited until night crept over the desert, cooling the dry, dusty air.

On August 2, at 1:30 A.M., when the intense heat of the day had sufficiently relented, Saddam ordered 100,000 Iraqi troops into Kuwait.

The Presidential Palace in Baghdad, situated on the Tigris River. Saddam ordered and directed the Iraqi invasion and occupation of Kuwait by radio communication from a well-fortified and elaborately equipped bunker deep below the palace.

A seemingly endless caravan of tanks, heavy artillery, and armored personnel carriers moved into the tiny desert country. The Iraqi troops encountered little resistance; by noon they had a firm grip on Kuwait City, the Kuwaiti capital.

The Kuwaiti ruler, or emir, Jaber Al-Ahmed Al-Sabah, was awakened by his cousin, the crown prince. Before sunrise, cloaked in long robes trimmed with gold, the emir and his family fled with all they could carry to the American embassy. The emir and those closest to him boarded a U.S. Army helicopter; the rest of the family and servants followed overland, making the one hour drive south to Saudi Arabia.

That afternoon, the Iraqi president explained the situation to King Hussein of Jordan in a telephone conversation: "We had to go in. . . . We were driven to that." He continued, "I am committed to withdrawal from Kuwait. It will start within days and last several weeks." It was Thursday, and the two leaders spoke of a possible summit on Sunday, with the leaders of Saudi Arabia, Yemen, Jordan, Iraq, and Egypt to resolve the matter.

Convinced that a negotiated Arab solution was possible, King Hussein immediately went to see Egypt's president, Hosni Mubarak, to relay Saddam's message, proposing a summit over the weekend in Jidda, Saudi Arabia, or Cairo, Egypt. It was important to Saddam, King Hussein emphasized, that none of the Arabs make hostile statements about the Iraqi action in Kuwait. Mubarak agreed.

King Hussein planned to go to Baghdad the following day to work out the terms. First, he and the Egyptian president placed a call to U.S. president George Bush, who was en route to meet with British prime minister Margaret Thatcher. "We can settle the crisis," said King Hussein. "We can deal with it. We just need a little time." He asked the U.S. president for 48 hours to secure a formal commitment from Saddam to withdraw from Kuwait and asked him not to put any pressure on the Arab leaders to criticize Iraq. "You've got it," replied Bush. "I'll leave it to you."

From Egypt, King Hussein returned to the Jordanian capital of Amman. Before leaving for Baghdad, he again phoned Mubarak, who said that he had spoken to Saudi Arabia's King Fahd to confirm the plans for the summit. Fahd had agreed to host the summit in Jidda on Sunday.

Saddam received the Jordanian king in Baghdad. "Will you leave Kuwait?" Hussein asked. "Yes," Saddam replied, "if my differences with the emirate can be settled." Saddam also had a request: "I don't want any members of the Al

Sabah family to attend the summit. I would prefer to negotiate an agreement with King Fahd. I've always had better
relations with him." He added, "And anyway, I've signed a
non-aggression pact with Saudi Arabia." The two leaders
then turned to the matter of the ongoing deliberations of
the Arab League, the organization of Arab states. Since
the day before, the Arab foreign ministers had been meeting in Cairo, where the Kuwaiti delegates were pushing
for a formal condemnation of Iraq's military action. Saddam warned, "Let's not scratch each other's eyes out. If
things move in that direction, I'll just say that Kuwait is part
of Iraq and annex it."

The Jordanian leader was optimistic as he left Baghdad
in the early afternoon. After all, Saddam had assured him
that he would begin to pull out of Kuwait on Sunday. His
optimism, however, was short-lived. At the airport in
Amman, the king took an urgent phone call from his foreign
minister informing him that the Egyptian foreign ministry
had just put out a statement condemning the Iraqis for
invading Kuwait.

King Hussein spent the rest of the day alone in his palace,
envisioning the turmoil that was now likely to befall the
region. He knew that Saddam now would not withdraw so
quickly. The Iraqi leader was a proud man who would not
be bullied, and he had a reputation in the region for keeping
his word. The Jordanian leader also knew that a crisis in any
part of the Middle East was bound to send shock waves
throughout the Arab world. He could already see it happening outside his window. In the streets of Amman, crowds
demonstrated in support of Saddam. Jordan was a poor
country, and more than half of its population was of Palestinian origin. Many Jordanians worked in Kuwait, Saudi
Arabia, and other wealthy Gulf countries, where they were
often looked down upon and treated with contempt.

Although Baghdad Radio had announced Saddam's
intention of withdrawing his troops from Kuwait on Sunday,
in the United States and Europe it was reported that Saddam

planned to take over Saudi Arabia's oil fields and possibly even the entire region. With 20 percent of the world's oil reserves beneath its soil, Saudi Arabia is crucial to the economic security of Europe and Japan. As the seriousness of the crisis sank in, Western media began to porray the Iraqi leader as a ruthless madman intent on world domination.

The Iraqi invasion should not have surprised anyone. For six months, Saddam had been threatening to use force if

Acutely aware of many complex and sensitive issues driving the politics of the Middle East, Jordan's King Hussein played an important mediating role following the Iraqi invasion of Kuwait.

The countries of the Persian Gulf region have known political struggle and instability for centuries, and many of the problems facing them today have existed for generations.

Kuwait did not negotiate an end to the territorial and financial disputes between the two countries. The territorial dispute was over the border between the two countries, which had never been formally demarcated. The financial dispute, Iraq claimed, was over the Iraqi war debt to Kuwait, accrued during Iraq's eight-year war with Iran, and over an Iraqi oil field from which Kuwait had been pumping valuable oil.

Kuwait brought this dispute to a critical juncture when it persisted in flooding the oil market in excess of the quota set by the Organization of Petroleum Exporting Countries

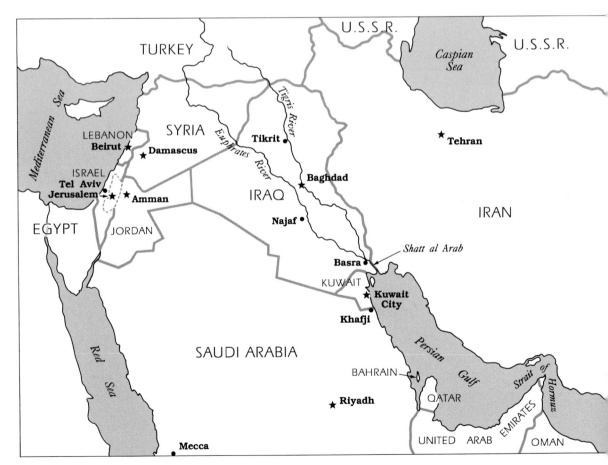

The Persian Gulf Region

(OPEC). This brought the price of oil down and severely debilitated Iraq's economy. Saddam believed that Kuwait, unlikely to make such a hostile and risky move without outside support, had done so with the encouragement of the United States, a long-time friend of Israel.

The United States seemed to be supporting the establishment of Jewish settlements in the Israeli-occupied territories on the West Bank of the Jordan River. The number of new settlements there had been increasing for some time but jumped dramatically with the crumbling of the Soviet Union in mid-1989 and the mass emigration of Soviet Jews to Israel. Saddam and much of the rest of the Arab world believed that the rapidly growing number of Jewish settlements on the West Bank would lead to its annexation and the expulsion of the region's Palestinians into Jordan, which Israeli prime minister Yitzhak Shamir claimed was really Palestine. Because of its strength and influence in the region, Iraq was the only Arab state capable of stopping Israel's gradual annexation of the occupied territories. Consequently, Israel had sought a way to neutralize Iraq's military might and concluded that one way to do this was to undermine Iraq's economic stability. Saddam thus reasoned that Kuwait was acting with the help of the United States and, indirectly, Israel, to destroy Iraq's economy.

The territory in the northeast of Kuwait had remained in dispute since Kuwait's creation by the British after World War I. Iraq, moreover, wanted to lease the two uninhabited islands at the south of Iraq's only outlet to the Persian Gulf, the Shatt Al-Arab waterway, but the Kuwaitis refused to lease them.

The roots of the border dispute between Iraq and Kuwait go back to two separate agreements signed by the British at the turn of the century. One was a secret agreement signed in 1899 between Britain and Sheikh Mubarak Al Sabah, an ancestor of the current Kuwaiti emir. At the time, Kuwait was merely a tiny pearl-fishing community, and Sheikh Mubarak Al Sabah reported to the Ottoman governor of

Basra Province. Iraq has long claimed that neither Kuwait's boundaries nor the sheikh's authority exceeded the town limits. Under international law, argue the Iraqis, he had no authority to reach accords with sovereign states.

The second agreement was reached with the Ottoman Empire in 1913, when the British recognized Kuwait as a district of Basra Province. Iraq has based its claims to Kuwait on this agreement since 1921, when Iraq was re-constituted by the British as a monarchy consisting of the provinces of Mosul, Baghdad, and Basra. Because sovereignty over Basra then passed officially from the Ottoman Empire to Iraq, Iraqis claimed that Kuwait was therefore an integral part of Iraq.

The dispute between Iraq and Kuwait is long standing and complex. Moreover, few Westerners are well enough acquainted with the history and culture of the Arab world to assess the arguments on both sides. But a basic outline of the dispute is helpful in understanding the points of contention.

The Iraqi monarchy was established in 1921 by the British government, which named King Faisal as its head. Soon afterward, the British high commissioner in Baghdad drew the final lines of the Iraqi–Saudi Arabian border, which stretched 600 miles across the desert from the Persian Gulf all the way to Jordan. At the same time, the high commissioner created a new border for Kuwait, declaring it a separate state. The new border gave to Kuwait some 100 miles of coastline that Iraq viewed as its own. The Iraqis protested, and no official border was established. Then, following Iraqi independence in 1932, debate over the border issue intensified until 1958, when Britain finally said it would yield to Iraq's claim to Kuwait. A meeting was scheduled in London to work out the details, but 10 days before the meeting, there was a military coup in Iraq, and the meeting never took place. When Britain granted Kuwait its independence in 1961, Iraq's new president promptly

declared that Iraq intended to recover Kuwait and sent troops to the border. This precipitated a British military buildup in Kuwait, supported by Egypt, Syria, Saudi Arabia, and the United States.

Iraq backed down in the face of the daunting British-led coalition. But the Soviet Union, which maintained a close friendship with Iraqi president Abdul Karim Kassem, vetoed Kuwait's entry into the United Nations. Less than two years later, Kassem was killed during an uprising in Iraq, one that was encouraged by the British. The new government managed to stay in power just long enough to issue a joint communiqué with Kuwait, recognizing its sovereignty. The governing council, however, refused to ratify it. It was during this period that Britain was able to push through Kuwait's membership in the UN.

Kuwait's entry into the UN, however, was not the end of the dispute. As Kuwait's statehood slowly became a reality, the Iraqis, in principle, came to accept it. But the northeast border remained a question. In 1973 and again in 1976, while Saddam was vice-president, Iraq asserted its claim to the disputed territory. This led to talks with Kuwait on a permanent border demarcation. In 1980, after Saddam was president, these talks were interrupted by Iraq's war with Iran.

When the Iran-Iraq war ended in 1988, Saddam sought to resume the border negotiations with Kuwait, but the Kuwaiti leaders were reluctant. Saddam pressed harder, claiming that Kuwait had moved its border farther north to where it straddled the southern tip of Iraq's Rumaila oil field. Also, the day after Iraq's war with Iran ended, Kuwait raised its oil output by half, which dramatically decreased the price of oil on the world market. Kuwait continued this policy off and on for the next two years. Iraq's economy, in shambles after the war, was practically destroyed.

Kuwait then began to demand repayment of the debt Iraq incurred in the war with Iran. On one occasion during the war, as Saddam liked to remind the Kuwaitis, Iraq had lost many men as a direct result of its defense of Kuwait. There had been an Iranian-backed attempt on the emir of Kuwait's life, and Iraq had taken strong retaliatory measures. Some 1,500 Iraqi soldiers had died as a result. Moreover, it was generally understood in the region that Iraq fought the war with Iran on behalf of all the Arab states and, therefore, that Kuwait should be expected to share the costs.

In 1990, despite these arguments, Kuwait continued to flood the oil market, and the price of oil dropped from $18 to $11 a barrel, causing Iraq to lose a full third of its income. In the spring and summer of 1990, Saddam repeatedly warned that he would resort to force if the Kuwaitis did not lower their oil production to conform to the OPEC quota. When they refused, the Iraqi president decided to take military action to destroy what he perceived as a Kuwaiti-U.S.-Israeli conspiracy.

Until very late in the game, Saddam did not believe that the United States would get involved in the dispute between Iraq and Kuwait. He reportedly believed that after the U.S. debacle in Vietnam the American people had no stomach for war halfway across the globe, especially where the United States was not directly threatened. That Saddam was gravely mistaken quickly became apparent on August 6, when Bush dispatched U.S. troops and warships to the Gulf region. Bush called the maneuver Operation Desert Shield.

During the fall and winter of 1990–91, Saddam Hussein and George Bush engaged in a heated conflict that became known as the Gulf crisis. On both sides, soldiers, having left their loved ones behind, stood ready to face their enemies while their leaders hurled ultimatums at each other and portrayed the struggle as one of good against evil, each claiming that God was on his side. It remained to be seen whether, when the Gulf crisis became the Gulf war, the conflict would be what Saddam had predicted—"the mother of all battles."

Local men rest on a hill above the town of Tikrit, located in northern Iraq on the banks of the Tigris River. Saddam was born in a mud house in Tikrit in 1937 and adopted the many customs of the region's patriarchal tribal society.

2

صُدّام حُسَين

Genesis

SADDAM HUSSEIN AL-TIKRITI was born on April 28, 1937, into a poor family in a mud house on the outskirts of Tikrit, a small Iraqi town on the Tigris River just north of Baghdad. The name Saddam, which means "He Who Faces the Aggressor," was given to him by his paternal uncle. The boy's father had died shortly before he was born. In accordance with Arab custom, Saddam's second name, Hussein, was his father's first name. As a last name, many people in the Middle East either take the name of their birthplace or that of their tribe. Saddam's last name, Al-Tikriti, means "from Tikrit."

Tikritis had a reputation for being brave and skillful fighters. Many Tikritis joined the army; for the poorer classes, joining the army was often the only way to get ahead. Tikritis filled the ranks of the Iraqi officer corps. After the 13th-century Mongol conquest of Baghdad, Mongols settled in Tikrit, and the conventional wisdom in Iraq is that all Tikritis have Mongol blood, the blood of some of history's greatest warriors.

Iraqi army officers pose outside Baghdad's Royal Palace (after 1958 known as the Presidential Palace) in the early 1930s. Many Tikritis, born into poverty, joined the army because enlisting was one way to escape their otherwise seemingly hopeless circumstances.

Tikritis were also very religious. Their spiritual, moral, and practical guide was the Koran, the holy book of the religion of Islam, which was founded by the prophet Muhammad in the 7th century A.D. in Mecca and Medina, cities far to the south on the Arabian Peninsula. Devout practitioners of their faith, they were known to be kind and generous to strangers despite their clannishness and the poverty they suffered.

Saddam's ancestors were probably nomads, desert bedouin from the Arabian Peninsula, who had emigrated to Tikrit, settling down and becoming farmers. For centuries, during times of drought in the desert, bedouin tribes—the first actually to call themselves Arabs, because their language was called Arabic—had been immigrating to the fringes of the Arabian desert, which reached north all the way to Syria and Iraq. They sometimes raided the settlements, sometimes joined them. Thus, over centuries the region had slowly become Arabized, with the desert tribes mixing with the people in the settlements.

Tikriti men wore the *kaffieh*, a large square of white or checkered head cloth, and they usually carried rifles or pistols when they went out. Tikriti women covered themselves with an *abbayah*, a black robe, from head to toe. In the villages and towns, women were expected to keep to their separate quarters with the children, never coming into contact with men other than relatives or a husband. A woman's status after she grew up depended solely on that of her husband's and the place he accorded her within the home. Often, he took other wives, as was the custom. By law a man was allowed to have four wives. If a woman became widowed and did not have any money, she and her children were taken in by other relatives until she found another husband. When Saddam's father died, his mother was taken in by her late husband's brother, who married her, in the village of Shawish, near Tikrit.

There, Saddam spent the first years of his life, helping with chores in the small family compound built from mud bricks. There was probably no electricity, and, wood being scarce, cooking was done mainly on a kerosene stove. Not far away was the desert, with ocher-colored sand blowing beneath a chalk-blue sky. Crops such as date palms, wheat, barley, corn, watercress, and melons were raised along the river with the help of irrigation, creating a splendid panorama of lush green that under the brilliant sunlight contrasted dramatically with the pale hues of the surrounding desert.

In 1941 there was an uprising in Iraq against the monarchy and British rule. The revolt lasted for several months. Saddam's mother told him stories about British treachery after the end of World War I, when the British had persuaded the Arabs to fight alongside them during the war against Germany's ally, the Ottoman Empire, which was ruled from Constantinople (now Istanbul), a city just north of Iraq. As a result, the Ottoman Empire had been brought to an end, but the British Empire had taken its place. Because these stories helped shape Saddam's views and actions in later life, it can be helpful to delve into the history of the region as it is taught and learned by those who live in that part of the world.

The Turks of the Ottoman Empire had occupied Iraq since the early 16th century, when they had begun their conquest of the Arab nation (the collective name for the countries that are predominantly Arab and Islamic) extending south to the Arabian Peninsula and east across northern Africa to Morocco. The Turks ruled the Arabs for four centuries. The Arab peoples had first been united under the Islamic Empire beginning in the early 7th century by the prophet Muhammad and by his successors, the caliphs. After Muhammad died, the seat of the caliphate was moved from Mecca to Damascus and, during the 8th century, to Baghdad. At its peak, the Islamic Empire stretched all the way from India to Morocco and Spain.

While Europe was slowly emerging from the Dark Ages, Baghdad was the center of a flourishing civilization, producing many of the world's foremost medical doctors, engineers, astronomers, mathematicians, philosophers, and artists. In 1258, invading Mongol hordes destroyed the city, carrying out a massacre that was said to turn the Tigris first bright red with blood and then black with ink when the Mongols dumped whole libraries into the river.

Never fully recovering from the Mongol invasion, Iraq and the Islamic Empire went into decline, and it was not difficult for the Turks, who were recent converts to Islam, to conquer the Arab nation in the 16th century, creating an Islamic Empire under the Ottoman dynasty. There were no borders separating the Arab peoples, and for purposes of administration the Turks kept the Arab system of provinces. Iraq was divided into four provinces: Mosul in the north, Baghdad in the center, Basra in the southwest, and Mohamarra (now Khuzistan) in the southeast.

While Iraq lay in squalor, the splendor of the Turkish court in Constantinople grew to dazzling proportions, recalling the glory of the former Abbasid court in Baghdad. Then, in 1914, as World War I raged in Europe, the Ottoman Empire entered the war on the side of Germany. Seeing a chance to rid themselves of the Ottoman yoke, many Arab leaders sided with Germany's enemy Britain. What began as an alliance against the Turks, however, soon amounted to the occupation by Britain and France of virtually all Arab lands. In order to bring about its alliance with Arab leaders, Britain made numerous promises of eventual Arab independence, many of which it ended up breaking. One such broken promise was made to Sherif Hussein, the desert ruler of the Hejaz, a wide strip of mountainous land on the Arabian Peninsula's west. The traditional guardian of Mecca, the holy city of Islam, Sherif Hussein claimed to be a direct descendant of the prophet Muhammad. The sherif's family were the Hashemites, descendants of the leading branch of Muhammad's Koreish tribe. The British promised to make Sherif Hussein the ruler of an area to include the Arabian Peninsula, Iraq, Syria, and Palestine. Great Britain broke this pledge two years later, in 1917, however, when it secretly agreed instead to establish a Jewish homeland in Palestine.

After the war, the British betrayed Sherif Hussein again, allowing the province of Hejaz, along with most of the Arabian Peninsula, to be taken over by the Saudis, who were primarily bedouin raiders living in the Nejd, the center of the Arabian Peninsula. The Saudis had long been allies of the British, who gave them weapons in exchange for helping to weaken the Ottoman rule in the Persian Gulf and the Red Sea.

With the formation of this new Saudi kingdom, tribal leaders in the Arabian Peninsula were sent into exile. Among these exiled leaders was Sherif Hussein. In compensation for having broken their agreements with him earlier, the British made two of his sons the kings of Transjordan and of Iraq. Transjordan (today called Jordan) was a strip of land north of the Hejaz, flanked on the west by Palestine, on the north by Syria, and on the east by Iraq.

Faisal I, son of the tribal leader Sherif Hussein, was named king of Iraq in 1921 by the British. A tough Arab nationalist committed to achieving Iraq's independence and the return of Kuwait to Iraq, Faisal fell out of favor with the British. He was killed in 1933.

A bustling Baghdad street in the early 1930s. Saddam left home before reaching his teens, moved to Tikrit, and then settled in Baghdad, Iraq's capital city, where he lived with his uncle and attended secondary school.

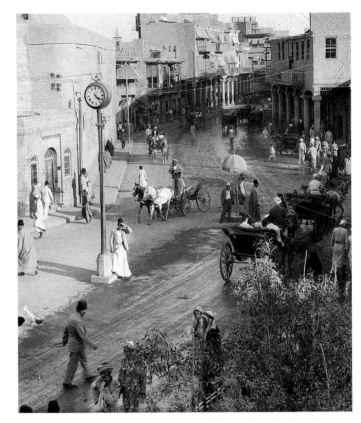

Sherif Hussein's sons became King Abdullah of Transjordan, grandfather of Jordan's King Hussein, and King Faisal of Iraq. By bringing in outsiders to rule, the British hoped to keep Iraq dependent on Britain. In Iraq, where there was oil and, unlike other Gulf states, a sizable population, a degree of control was vital to British interests. Before long, however, Faisal demanded both the return of Kuwait and Iraqi self-determination. In 1932, Britain granted Iraq its independence.

When King Faisal died in 1933, his doctors and family claimed that it was at the hands of the British. After his father's death, King Ghazi reasserted Iraq's claim to Kuwait. Then, in 1938, his automobile crashed into a high-voltage electrical pole, killing him. An investigation concluded that the British had arranged the accident. During

Saddam Hussein's youth, with King Faisal II still a child, Iraq was ruled by a regent chosen by Britain.

When the German dictator Adolf Hitler began to bomb Britain in the spring of 1940, many Arabs sided with Germany, the enemy of their former colonial ruler. Soon, the Iraqis were inspired to revolt against the British-supported monarchy. Several of Saddam's relatives were killed and had their homes burned down by the British during the uprising. Saddam's uncle Khairallah Talfah took part in the 1941 revolt, and Saddam's mother never tired of telling the little boy about her brother's exploits. She also told him about how his great-grandfather and his two brothers, aged 14 and 16, had died fighting alongside the British for independence from the Turks only to be betrayed after the war. Like most Iraqis, the family hated the British imperialists.

During school vacation, Saddam's cousin, Adnan Khairallah, who would serve as Iraq's minister of defense during the Iran-Iraq war, often came from Tikrit to visit. One day he told Saddam about how he was learning to read and write at school, and he drew his name in the dirt in front of the mud-brick house. Enchanted by the idea of learning arithmetic and reading and writing, Saddam begged his mother to send him to school in Tikrit with his cousin. But the family was poor; Saddam was meant to be a farmer when he grew up. There was no need for Saddam to learn to read or write. Her answer was no.

Already, Saddam was considered a leader among the neighborhood boys, setting a moral example by giving away his clothes to those who were needier than he was. Whenever the chattering and laughter of a group of boys was heard in the street, it is said that the villagers would remark, "There goes Saddam." Saddam's favorite pastime was riding his horse across the desert plain.

One night, when Saddam was 9 or 10, he crept out of bed after everyone was asleep and gathered up his few belongings into a bundle. He walked two hours to the village of Al Fatha, where he sought out some relatives who were

Because she was widowed before her son was born, Saddam's mother left it to the boy's paternal uncle to name the child, in accordance with Arab custom. The name he chose, Saddam, means "He Who Faces the Aggressor."

watchmen. He asked them for help in getting to his uncle's home in Tikrit so he could go to school. Saddam seemed so determined to go that they gave him a pistol and arranged for a taxi to take him to Tikrit. (There were bandits on the roads at the time, and boys learned to use guns very early in life.) In Tikrit, Saddam was welcomed by his uncle Hajj Khairallah, who thereafter looked after him. As the senior male member of the extended family, or tribe, Hajj Khairallah was considered to be its sheikh, or leader, and was often called upon to mediate disputes. His decisions were final.

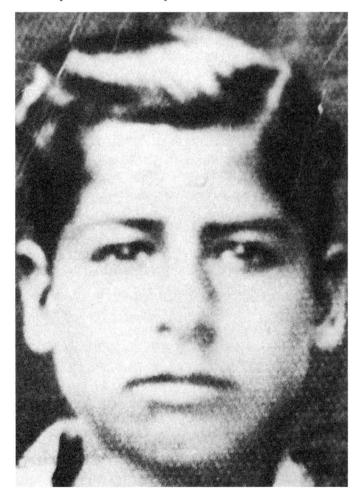

As a teenager during the late 1940s and 1950s, Saddam witnessed the growing tension between the countries of the Arab world and the newly created state of Israel. The seeds of Saddam's Arab nationalism were thus planted early.

In and around Tikrit, Hajj Khairallah was known as an intellectual. He wrote books and articles and was considered very learned in matters of history and religion. He had once studied to be a teacher and attended the military academy. A year after Saddam arrived, Hajj Khairallah moved to Baghdad, leaving his nephew in Tikrit to finish primary school.

Perhaps Saddam wanted to stay behind to be near his horse, which awaited him in the village on holidays. Two years later, when Saddam was in the fifth grade, he learned that his horse had died, and the world closed in on him. His hand was paralyzed for 10 days, and he had to be treated with local folk remedies. When Saddam recovered, he joined his uncle in Baghdad, where he attended secondary school.

Around that time, a political event took place that shook the Arab world. In fact, its effect on Arabs was more powerful than anything that had happened since World War I. The event was the declaration of the state of Israel by the Jews in Palestine on May 14, 1948. The United States was the first nation to recognize the new state.

Iraq immediately closed down its only oil pipeline, which ran to the Mediterranean through Haifa, a port city in today's northwest Israel, and, like most other Arab states, sent troops to fight against Israel. Arab boys switched from playing war between the Germans and the British to war between the Arabs and the Jews. This first Arab-Israeli war was short-lived, however, with the Arabs having to withdraw in defeat and humiliation.

Throughout his life, Saddam, whose best subject in school was history, would be moved by an intense desire to avenge this terrible defeat and to return the Arab world to the greatness it once knew. He may have been born in a mud house, but the humble circumstances of his birth would not stop him from pursuing that dream nor, in fact, from becoming one of the most powerful leaders in the Arab world.

As the Arab nationalist movement gained momentum, Saddam became increasingly interested and active in politics. When Britain used Iraqi air bases to launch an attack on Egypt in 1956, Iraqis protested, and Saddam joined the demonstrations.

3

صَدَّام حُسَين

Exodus

THE CREATION OF THE STATE OF ISRAEL was the result of a 19th-century Jewish nationalist movement called Zionism. With the advent of the Zionist movement, Jewish nationhood became a political objective for an increasing number of Jews. Zionists advocated the creation of a Jewish state on the land inhabited by the Jews before their dispersal under the Roman Empire in A.D. 70. For some Zionists, this meant the restoration not only of the Jewish territory from the time of the Romans but of all the lands where biblical Jewish history had unfolded. That included everything between the Nile River in Egypt and the Euphrates in Iraq, which in the Book of Genesis God promises to Abraham's descendants. In the early 20th century, Zionists began a campaign to expel the Palestinian Arabs from Palestine and thereby create a strictly Jewish state.

Notwithstanding Britain's earlier promise to the Arabs, the British foreign secretary Arthur Balfour secretly wrote a letter to a prominent

British Zionist leader named Baron Lionel Walter Roth-schild (the cousin of the French Zionist leader Edmond de Rothschild) in 1917. The letter, in which he promised the Jews a homeland in Palestine, came to be known as the Balfour Declaration. The British also promised to make Palestine a Jewish commonwealth once the Jews had achieved a majority population. Consequently, the Zionists began their campaign to drive the Palestinians out. One tactic in this effort was an organized Jewish boycott of Arab markets, which weakened the local economy and forced Palestinians to sell their land cheaply.

During the 1930s, this led to a massive Arab revolt, and Britain decided to place a limit on further Jewish immigration and the purchase of Arab land by Jews. Also, Britain announced its intention to create a Palestinian rather than a Jewish state within 10 years. Zionists were outraged that the British had broken their promise, even though they had come nowhere near achieving a Jewish majority in Palestine, and relations between them were strained for years, with organized Jewish gangs terrorizing the British as well as the Arabs. When World War II broke out, however, the Zionists persuaded the British to create special Jewish military units. After the war, these units became the Jewish, and eventually, the Israeli army.

After the war ended, the difficulties of establishing a secular Palestinian state in the presence of a powerful Jewish army prompted Britain in 1947 to announce that it would abandon the Palestinian mandate to the United Nations (UN) the following year. The UN then voted for the partition of Palestine into two states—one Jewish and one Arab.

The Arabs bitterly rejected this proposal. They favored a secular Palestine, where Muslims, Christians, and Jews could coexist. They argued, moreover, that Jews would receive more than half of Palestine, including all the best farmland, even though they owned only 6 percent of the land and made up only a third of the population. Most of those Jews had been in Palestine less than 30 years.

Even though the partition arrangement greatly favored the Zionists, they were not satisfied any more than the Arabs were. The Zionists had once sought not only all of Palestine but southern Lebanon, southwest Syria, and most of Transjordan as well. However, knowing that the Palestinians would reject the partition, the Zionists embraced it in order to give the appearance that they were eager to compromise and make peace.

Meanwhile, Zionist groups launched an extremely violent campaign to drive the remaining native Arab population out of Palestine. One stunning incident was the massacre at the Arab village of Deir Yassin, in which Zionists murdered 254 people in April 1948. The massacre was carried out under the command of future Israeli prime minister Menachem Begin, then the leader of the Zionist terrorist group Irgun. Also participating were the Stern Gang and the elite Zionist force, the Palmach. The Zionists entered Deir Yassin during the night when the villagers were asleep and went from house to house, killing and maiming men, women, and children. Many witnesses recounted horrifying tales of the brutality and slaughter at the hands of the Zionists.

Although there had been sporadic terrorist actions by the Palestinians, their leadership was not calling for violent solutions. Still, following the declaration of the state of Israel, full-scale fighting broke out between the Arabs and the Zionists. The Palestinian Arabs were aided by troops from neighboring Arab nations, but Israel, heavily financed by Jews abroad, emerged victorious, expanding its borders even beyond those established by the partition plan. The majority of the Arab population of Palestine, estimated at more than 1 million, was displaced by the Israeli victory. Some 400,000 Arabs, many of them Christians, remained in Israel after the war, but these people found they were stripped of their rights as citizens, even though they still made up nearly half of Israel's population. Israel had no plans for a constitution.

A candidate for Israeli prime minister in 1949, Menachem Begin, casts his vote in the election. The previous year, the Irgun, a militant Zionist group of which Begin was the leader, massacred more than 250 people in the Arab village of Deir Yassin.

Following the creation of the state of Israel in 1948, Zionists, whose principal goal was the creation of a Jewish state, stepped up their effort to expel Arabs from Palestine. As a result, hundreds of thousands of Palestinian Arabs fled their homes and set up camps such as this one in Lebanon.

Despite their humiliating defeat by Israel, many Arabs redoubled their resolve to fight Zionism and European colonialism. (After the war, the United States, as Israel's main supporter, to some extent replaced the British as the hated colonial power in the Arab world.) One such Arab was Gamal Abdul Nasser, a young Egyptian army officer who served in the disastrous Arab campaign in Palestine. In 1952, well versed in the Arab nationalist ideas of the Syrian Baathis, Nasser carried out a military coup in Egypt against the British-supported monarchy and became Egypt's president.

On July 27, 1956, Nasser announced that he was nationalizing the Suez Canal—meaning that he was declaring it the property of Egypt. Nasser was a strong spokesman for the pan-Arabist movement. Pan-Arabism is based on the notion that by virtue of their common language, culture, and history, the Arab countries actually constitute a single nation united in the struggle against Israel and Western colonialism. Nasser declared that valuable natural resources such as oil and the Suez Canal—which was jointly owned by the French and the British and heavily relied upon as a vital waterway between the Mediterranean and Red seas— rightfully belonged to Egypt and would not remain in the hands of foreign powers. For the Arab world to regain its political and economic dignity and influence, Nasser believed, Arabs had to take control of what truly belonged to them. His words, "Humiliation is over," spread euphoria throughout the Arab world.

Saddam, 19 years old at the time and a student in Baghdad, was swept up in that pan-Arabist euphoria. Like other Arabs, Saddam was impressed with Nasser's bold declaration and was inspired by the notion of restoring greatness to the Arab world through organized Arab unity.

Then, on October 27, the Israeli Army invaded the Sinai Peninsula, conquering the Suez Canal within four days. Israel was quickly joined by British and French forces. The United States, the Soviet Union, and all Arab nations criticized this British-French-Israeli attack on Egypt, and the UN, under pressure from the Soviets, in the spring forced Israel to pull its troops out of Egypt, turning the military defeat into a political victory for Nasser.

The 1956 war had an important impact on Saddam Hussein. During the attack on Egypt, British troops had used Iraqi air bases, which triggered Iraqi demonstrations against the British-backed monarchy. These demonstrations were organized by the Iraqi branch of the Arab Baath (Renaissance) party, which was founded in 1947 by Michel Aflaq, a young Syrian Christian and Arab nationalist, and two Muslim friends. Saddam was one of those who joined the protests. Soon the young student embraced the Baath ideology with a passion and joined the party.

Although the Arab Baath was socialist and secular, Islam, the religion of the majority of Arabs, played an important spiritual and practical role in the party's ideology. Still, an Arab, as the Baath defined the term, was anyone who spoke Arabic and considered himself or herself an

Arab, regardless of one's religion. Created during the most traumatic period in recent Arab history, the Arab Baath party was also strongly pan-Arabist and dedicated to the restoration of Palestine.

At the time of the Suez crisis, when Saddam joined the Baath party and became a militant Arab nationalist, the Baathis in the Syrian government were working toward a union of Syria and Egypt as a first step toward the reunification of the Arab nation. In early 1958, Israeli fears materialized when the two countries formed the United Arab Republic. They were soon joined by Yemen, a country on the southern tip of the Arabian Peninsula. At the same time, Britain attempted to counter the Arab-nationalist movement by promoting the union of Jordan and Iraq, the rulers of which were cousins.

The matter of Kuwait, which was still under British mandate, then became a key issue. Iraq's prime minister, pressing for the return of Kuwait to Iraq, announced that he would detail publicly the historical and legal reasons for his country's claim on the territory, but the British sent word for him to wait, saying they had decided to approve Kuwait's accession. He was invited to London in late July 1958 to finalize the arrangement. Shortly before the meeting, however, the Iraqi king and his entire government were massacred in a military coup, and General Abdul Karim Kassem declared Iraq a republic.

Kassem's was a bloody regime that, like the monarchy, did not allow any opposition political activity, and soon the Baathis, whose Arab nationalist ideals conflicted with those of Kassem's Communist supporters, were being hunted down and persecuted. In March 1959, the Communists carried out a massacre of thousands of Baathis in Mosul. During a so-called peace festival, the Communist party called on its members to rid the country of nationalism, and there was a frenzy of killing. A gallows was set up in the street, and mostly Baathis were dragged there. General Kassem did nothing to stop the massacre. In fact, he allowed

General Abdul Karim Kassem (center) led a military coup that toppled the Iraqi monarchy in 1958. Kassem's quickly became a violent and repressive regime that Saddam, as a new member of the Iraqi Baath party, was committed to overthrowing.

other massacres as well in the Iraqi cities of Baghdad, Basra, and Kirkuk. As a result, the Iraqi Baath party decided to assassinate Kassem.

During the summer of 1959, Saddam was on vacation in Tikrit when a government official was killed there. Saddam was charged with the murder and thrown in prison. There he demonstrated a capability for leadership. The Baathis were routinely subjected to floggings and electrical shocks, and in the face of these punishments, Saddam worked hard to restore morale to his fellow Baathi prisoners. He also managed to persuade some of the guards to allow some of his free comrades to take refuge during the day inside the prison.

In the fall, the charges against Saddam were dropped, and he was set free. The party then gave him the task of painting slogans on walls at night. Soon, however, they set before him a far more important task—and one many considered a great honor: He was one of five chosen to assassinate Kassem.

On the appointed day, Saddam and his comrades took up posts on Rashid Street, Baghdad's main thoroughfare, along which Kassem and his entourage traveled every day. Saddam's job was to cover the others while they approached Kassem's automobile with machine guns. When he heard the first shots, Saddam became so excited that he ran up to Kassem's car and joined in the firing. Shooting into the windows, they shouted, "This is for Mosul! This is for Baghdad! For Basra! For Kirkuk!"

Two of the bodyguards were killed, but Kassem survived. In the retreat, Saddam was hit by a bullet in the leg. The following morning, he and a friend removed the bullet with a razor blade and scissors. Saddam filled himself with antibiotics meant for a sore throat and then went to school so as not to arouse suspicions. He was in his last year of high school. That afternoon, when Saddam heard that the others had been arrested, he rushed home, packed his belongings, and fled. Fifteen minutes later, the house was raided by the police.

After spending the night at a relative's house, Saddam started out for Tikrit, dressed as a bedouin in tattered robes and taking great care to hide his wound and not to limp when there were people around. On the outskirts of Baghdad, he bought a horse. Three days later, he arrived at a village across the river from where his family lived, near Tikrit. After nightfall, he left his horse behind and swam across the river with his clothes tied in a bundle, his knife held tightly between his teeth. As he would later tell this story, the water was so cold and the current so strong that for a moment he doubted he would make it.

When he finally reached the other side, Saddam put on his wet clothes and, shivering with cold, knocked on the door of a house. After he convinced the family that he was not a thief, they let him enter. While his clothes were drying, they noticed his leg wound and decided to turn him over to the police. But he talked them out of this by convincing them that he had received the wound in a tribal feud.

The following day, Saddam was able to find his brother Addham, who was a caretaker at a nearby school, and together they went to their mother's house. The police had already been there looking for him. From Tikrit, party members helped him across the desert to Syria, now part of the United Arab Republic, where the Baathis controlled the government. Saddam stayed in Damascus for three months, meeting with the National Baathi leadership. The highest level in the party was the National Command, located in Damascus, consisting of members from different Arab states, representing the entire Arab nation. The party was divided into regional commands of single countries, such as Iraq, subordinate to the National Command.

In the spring of 1960, Saddam flew to Cairo, the capital of Egypt and the center of Arab nationalism. There, Saddam enrolled in law school and became active in Cairo's regional Baath party headquarters. Soon he became a student leader for the party.

Saddam quickly rose through the party ranks in Cairo. First, he became an elected member of the Egyptian party division, then of the Branch Command, and then, in 1961, of the Regional Command. When he was not studying or carrying out party duties, Saddam, always interested in history, traveled throughout Egypt, visiting archaeological sites. He also played chess regularly and had many friends.

While he was in Cairo, he was betrothed through the mail to his cousin Sajida, a schoolteacher and Khairallah Talfah's daughter. Her father said the couple could get married when Saddam returned to Baghdad.

In February 1963, the Baath party came to power in Iraq, and Kassem was immediately executed. A relative of Saddam's from Tikrit, Ahmad Hassan Al Bakr, who was the

Merchants display their wares at a Baghdad bazaar. In February 1963, the Baath party came to power in Iraq, and Saddam returned to Baghdad from Egypt, to which he had fled after playing a leading role in an unsuccessful attempt on Kassem's life.

secretary general of the Baath party, became prime minister. The Baathis went on a rampage, jailing and executing Communists.

Then, a Kurdish insurrection led by Sheikh Mustafa Barzani broke out in the north. The Kurds were a non-Arab people living in parts of Syria, Iraq, Turkey, Iran, and the republic of Caucasus in the Soviet Union. They had never had their own country, but after World War I the British had promised them one. This promise was never kept, and the Kurds continued to struggle for a homeland.

During the 1950s, Israel had formed alliances with the Kurds and other non-Arabs in the region in order to drive a wedge between Arab and non-Arab Muslims. By feeding

the historical rivalries, Israel meant to keep the Muslims divided and weak, much as the British had done earlier. As the only nearby Arab state with both oil wealth and a large population, Iraq had become a primary concern for Israel, which had begun supplying Iraqi Kurds with weapons when Kassem had come to power. When the Baath party took over, Israel felt an even greater need to undermine Iraq's stability by arming the Kurds.

When he returned to Baghdad immediately after the coup, Saddam was put in charge of the Central Peasants Bureau. He found the party in Iraq plagued by paranoia and terror. He openly criticized the party and predicted that the Baathi revolution would not last long in Iraq. There were several attempts on his life.

The Syrian pan-Arabist and Baath party cofounder, Michel Aflaq, was extremely impressed with the young Saddam during a trip to Baghdad. Later, to an Arab jour- nalist, Aflaq said of him, "I was surprised to hear such well-developed opinions in his criticism of the actions of the Regional Command at the time. He also gave a clear picture of what proper party leadership should be. My first and lasting impression was of equilibrium, calmness, rationality and clarity of thought. This is rare in revolutionary action, at least in our Arab milieu, because hasty emotionalism has often been one of the negative characteristics of our revolutionaries." Saddam, said Aflaq, was the leader who made the party strong in the next stage. He saw the young Iraqi as someone with reason, courage, initiative and, most important, nerves of steel.

A little more than nine months after they came to power, the Baathis were ousted from the government just as Saddam had predicted. Saddam was put in charge of the party's paramilitary arm and instructed to plan for another takeover of the government the following year. The plan was for him to enter the Presidential Palace at the head of a commando team during a cabinet meeting and machine-gun the entire government.

On September 4, 1964, the day before the coup was to take place, the plot was discovered and Saddam was sought by the police. The party ordered Saddam to go to Damascus, Syria. However, having come to the conclusion that it had been a mistake to flee the country in 1959, Saddam disobeyed the order. To raise morale, he brazenly announced over the radio that he was in Baghdad and still working for the party. Soon, he was again arrested and imprisoned.

In prison, the savage torturing of the Baathis was resumed, and once more Saddam worked to keep up their spirits. He also read a lot, organized a hunger strike to protest the inhumane conditions at the prison, managed to have some files smuggled in, and helped several men escape. He had married his cousin Sajida and was able to get permission for her to visit him once a week with their six-month-old son, Uday. Saddam remained in contact with the party through secret messages, often hidden in the baby's swaddling clothes.

Saddam had been in prison for nearly two years when he received word that the party was getting ready to overthrow the military regime and that he was needed outside. On July 23, 1966, Saddam persuaded the guards to allow him and his comrades to go to a restaurant on the way to court. On the pretext of going to the washroom, Saddam left the group and escaped through the back door.

Several important things had taken place in the party while Saddam had been in prison. First, he had been elected a member of the National Command. Until then, Al Bakr had been the sole Iraqi at the organization's national level. Then, on February 23, 1966, a group of Syrian army officers had led a coup within the party in Damascus, ousting Michel Aflaq, and claimed to be the new national leadership.

Saddam and his comrades refused to recognize the usurpers, causing a serious split in the party in Iraq. Saddam's faction then won a fiercely contested regional election, wresting control of the Iraqi party from the new leadership in Syria. Al Bakr was elected secretary general, and Saddam, Al Bakr's deputy, was put in charge of the party's Baghdad branch. Before the elections, Saddam was so sick and weak from an attack of severe gastroenteritis that he thought he had cholera. Nevertheless, he insisted on attending an important meeting even though he had to be carried there. Unable to sit up, he spoke while lying down, impressing everyone with his extraordinary dedication.

Meanwhile, Israel had set the stage for world public opinion by triggering an incident that would cause outrage against the Arabs. In the spring of 1967, the Israeli army provoked the Syrians into firing on Israeli farmers, intruding on the Arab demilitarized zone below the Golan Heights. Then, two Israeli generals announced on the radio separately that Israel was planning to march on Damascus to overthrow the Syrian government. One of them added, taunting Nasser, that the Egyptians were too weak to come to Syria's aid.

His pride smarting, Nasser asked the UN peacekeeping forces to leave the Sinai and announced a blockade of Israel's southern port of Elat. Claiming preemptive action to avoid being attacked by the Arabs, Israel simultaneously attacked three Arab countries in June. Within six days, the Israelis occupied the Sinai Peninsula again, Syria's Golan Heights, where the Jordan River begins, and the West Bank in Jordan, including East Jerusalem, home to the Dome of the Rock mosque, Islam's third holiest site. Built on the rock from where Muhammad had reportedly risen to heaven, the Dome of the Rock was also on top of the Temple Mount, the remains of the Jewish temple destroyed by the Romans nearly 2,000 years earlier. The one visible wall, known as the Wailing Wall, is considered the holiest Jewish site.

Now, for the second time, Iraq sent troops to fight Israel, and once again the Arab forces were beaten back, suffering an even more humiliating defeat than they had experienced in 1948. The Palestinians in the occupied West Bank and Gaza were put under Israeli military law, and many of them became refugees for the second time. Upon entering Jerusalem, the Israelis immediately razed the Arab sector next to the mosque and bulldozed entire villages in the vicinity, extending the city limits to cover a fifth of the West Bank. Then, Israel annexed East Jerusalem and offered financial incentives to Jews who would settle in the occupied territories. The Israelis harassed the native Arabs, jailing their leaders without charges and deporting them. They destroyed homes for alleged political offenses and requisitioned Palestinian land for national security reasons.

Soon, Palestinian terrorists were hijacking planes, mainly in Europe and the Middle East, and orchestrating bomb attacks on innocent civilians in public places. In 1972, nine Israeli athletes and two coaches were killed at the Olympic Games in Munich, West Germany. Such terrorist incidents became increasingly common throughout the 1970s. The

A Palestinian family flees the Israeli-occupied West Bank for Jordan in 1967. That year, the Israeli Army dealt Arab forces a humiliating defeat in only six days of fighting, and Saddam watched in horror as the plight of the Palestinians became ever more desperate.

Israeli Occupation in 1967

This map shows the areas claimed by Israel in the 1967 Arab-Israeli war. Israel returned the Sinai Peninsula to Egypt in 1979 as part of its obligation under a peace treaty signed at Camp David, Maryland, in March of that year, but continued to occupy the West Bank, Golan Heights, and Gaza Strip.

terrorists, trained mostly in Lebanon, Syria, and Iraq, were received in most Arab capitals as freedom fighters.

The Baathis in Iraq watched in horror as Israel expanded in the direction of Baghdad during the 1967 war. Saddam began to dream of building a mighty Arab army, worthy of the West's and of Israel's respect. He vowed to turn Iraq into a modern state and harness Iraq's oil wealth to the Baathi ideals. His goal was self-sufficiency, first for Iraq and eventually for the entire Arab nation. It was a dream for which Baathis were willing to kill and even die, and they were ready to make their bid for power.

By the 1960s, Saddam had shown extraordinary courage and resolve and had emerged as a Baath party leader. When the Baathis were ousted, only nine months after they came to power, Saddam set about plotting to retake the government for his party.

4

صّدام حُسـين

Numbers

SADDAM ROSE AT 2:30 IN THE MORNING on July 17, 1968. There was much to do, and he wanted to get an early start. He began by bringing out all of the weapons and uniforms he had hidden in his house. His wife Sajida helped in the preparations, as did their son Uday, who ran around the room picking up hand grenades from the floor, bringing them one by one to his father as if they were toys.

Once Saddam was at Al Bakr's house and the group had changed into uniforms, Al Bakr led the way to the palace in a white Mercedes. Saddam and his comrades followed in a truck. Before dawn they arrived at the outer gates to the Republican Palace, where the commander on duty let them in. The Baathis commandeered a squadron of tanks parked under the trees. When they began starting them up, the soldiers in the adjoining barracks ran to see what was happening. In the confusion, Saddam persuaded one of them, after his brother Barzan had knocked him down and taken his machine gun away, that he should join them. Saddam told him they were putting down a coup. "God bless you," said the man, unaware of the irony of his situation, and offered to drive the tank.

At dawn on July 17, 1968, Saddam and Barzan, wearing lieutenant uniforms, rolled toward the Republican Palace in Baghdad on the back of that tank. They passed through the inner gates to the palace with the other tanks, shooting until the president came out and surrendered.

Ahmad Hassan Al Bakr became Iraq's new president. During his years in the underground, Al Bakr had come to rely heavily on Saddam, and now many people saw the two men as equal partners in power.

The Baathis quickly set about filling government positions. Al Bakr also became president of the Revolutionary

In a July 1968 coup, the Iraqi Baath party regained control of Iraq, and Saddam, now 31 years old, became vice-president. Here he is pictured with Iraqi president Ahmad Hassan Al Bakr (seated left of Saddam) and other Iraqi officials.

Command Council (RCC), the supreme authority in the new government. Its members in the future would all be chosen by the party, but for now the Baathis shared power with certain army officers who had supported the coup. The post of prime minister went to General Abdul-Razaq Al Najif, the wily and powerful head of military intelligence, who had forced his way into the ranks of the revolutionaries only an hour before the coup was launched. Saddam became vice-president as well as the number two man in the RCC, although this was not publicly announced for more than a year.

Vice-president Saddam was 31 years old at the time of the coup and had spent all of his adult years working full-time for the party, mostly underground. Saddam and the Baathis had functioned as a clandestine movement for nearly two decades in Iraq, always acting with extreme caution. Now that the Baathis were in power, they continued to function largely as a secret organization.

Having attained his position in the new government by force, Al Najif settled in as prime minister with a 12-member personal security guard. Also for his own protection, he made certain that his men were put in charge of palace security and of the Republican Guard. From the start, he caused great embarrassment to the Baathis. One of the revolution's first slogans was "Arab Oil for the Arabs," yet the new prime minister was proposing that the National Petroleum Company, formed during Kassem's rule as a first step toward nationalization of the oil industry, be dissolved in favor of foreign oil interests. Saddam, who led the group that wanted to nationalize oil, did not sleep at night for the first two weeks after the coup, wondering what to do. His wife had never seen him so nervous.

Two weeks after the coup, Saddam instructed Barzan and five trusted comrades to help remove Al Najif. He then ordered the commander of the Tenth Brigade, who had supported the coup and whom he trusted, to have his men surround the inner perimeter of the palace. "If he tries to escape, I will kill him," Saddam said.

The commander then joined Saddam and several cabinet members and officers for lunch in the president's private dining room. Among them was Al Najif. They ate venison that one of the officers had brought back from a hunt. After lunch, Al Najif was invited to President Al Bakr's office for coffee, as planned. He sat with his back to the door, facing the president's enormous desk. Saddam, with Barzan and his group, entered, drawing their revolvers. Saddam held a gun to Al Najif's back and told him to put up his hands. The color draining from his face as the vice-president took his revolver away, Al Najif responded nervously, "I have four children." Saddam told Al Najif that nothing would happen to him if he did what he was told. "You know," he said, "you forced your way into this revolution, and you are a stumbling block for the party. We have paid for this revolution with our blood."

Al Najif was sent to Morocco, where he could cause no trouble for the new Iraqi government, and he was made an ambassador to keep up appearances. Saddam, with his hand on his gun inside his jacket pocket, accompanied Al Najif to the airport. Not until Al Najif was inside the plane did Saddam take his finger off the trigger. He then returned Al Najif's revolver and instructed one of the guards accompanying the former prime minister to return the bullets when they touched down in Morocco. Standing on the tarmac, Saddam watched the plane fade into the sky and breathed a sigh of relief—the revolution was safe.

There were resentful murmurings within the party that the Tikriti clique was running the government. Besides the president and Saddam, the chief of staff and many of the senior officials and army officers were from Tikrit. The criticism eventually prompted Saddam to drop Al Tikriti as a last name, becoming simply Saddam Hussein.

It was not until after Saddam was vice-president that he finally received his law degree. Soon after the coup, he enrolled at the university in Baghdad. He asked for no special privileges. In fact, many of his fellow students did not realize that their classmate was the vice-president; to maintain his anonymity he wore a disguise to class. During his underground years he had developed a knack for concealing his identity through the use of disguises. Now he frequently walked the streets in disguise so as to hear what the people thought of the government.

On November 30, 1971, the shah of Iran, Mohammad Reza Pahlavi, seized three Arab islands belonging to the United Arab Emirates at the south of the Persian Gulf. Not only did the islands have oil, but, more important, they were of great strategic importance because they controlled the Straits of Hormuz at the entrance to the Gulf. The Baathis saw the shah's move as foreign encroachment on the Arab nation and they broke relations with Iran over this incident. They also broke relations with the British for having encouraged the shah. The Baathis believed that if the Arabs had been united, Iran could never have got away with such aggression.

In the early 1970s, after the oil industry was nationalized, Iraq saw a dramatic increase in its oil revenue and was suddenly in a good position to make long-range plans to build roads, bridges, hospitals, schools, and factories. To do so, the Iraqi leader drew up a nationwide development program, including an extensive irrigation project to create more arable farmland. Baghdad, he believed, could be transformed into a great cosmopolitan city. Eager for his country to join the ranks of the great industrialized nations, Saddam signed a friendship treaty with the Soviet Union in order to bring Soviet technology to Iraq.

But Saddam thought it was important to balance this Soviet alliance with stronger ties to the West. In 1972 and

1975, Saddam traveled to France, signing important trade and cultural exchange agreements. He also arranged to sell Iraqi oil to France. Before long, France was selling advanced weapons to Iraq. Saddam would also have liked to reestablish diplomatic relations with the United States, broken during the 1967 war, but the United States had since increased its support for Israel and was also promoting the shah of Iran as the policeman of the Persian Gulf region.

Saddam's trips to France led to the sale of two nuclear reactors meant to provide Iraq with inexpensive energy. Israel then charged that the French had made a secret deal to help Iraq build an atomic bomb, thereby endangering Israel. It was true that the Iraqis were hoping to develop nuclear weapons, as India had already done and Pakistan was doing. They knew that Israel had them already. Nevertheless, Saddam could not help remarking that similar reactors, 78 of them in fact, had already been sold to other Third World countries, and no one had questioned those sales. He wryly remarked that if Iraq was able to produce 20 atomic weapons but remained a backward, underdeveloped country, Israel would not make any such fuss. Once Iraq became an industrialized country, he believed, it would no longer be possible for Israel to push the Arabs around with impunity.

In the spring of 1973, U.S. senator William Fulbright, chairman of the Senate Foreign Relations Committee, warned that growing dependence on Middle Eastern oil could lead to a U.S. takeover of the Arab oil states by force, adding, in an allusion to Israel, "We might not even have to do it ourselves, with militarily potent surrogates available in the region." Arabs were alarmed.

In October, Egypt and Syria made a surprise attack on Israel. Although Saddam and the other Baathis had not been asked to join, or even been alerted, they felt that it was their duty to join the fighting. Though Israel once more defeated the Arabs, it took Israel several weeks to gain the

Kurdish rebels in northern Iraq. Saddam devised a plan for Kurdish autonomy in 1970, but the Kurds rejected it and unleashed a civil war in 1974, when the plan was scheduled to go into effect. It was one year before the signing of the Algiers Accord stopped the flow of Iranian arms to the Kurds, ending the uprising.

victory, and its supposedly invincible defense line in the Sinai was penetrated. Although the Israelis managed to hold onto the occupied territories, the Arabs had put up a good fight.

In 1970, Saddam proposed a plan for Kurdish autonomy, meant to take effect as law in March 1974. The plan included provisions for the administration of Kurdish territory to pass into Kurdish hands and for a Kurdish parliament to be elected. Also, Iraq would have a mandatory Kurdish vice-president. Unlike Turkey and Iran, where the Kurds have not been allowed to speak their own language, Iraq ensured that Kurdish would be the first language in the local Kurdish government, schools, and universities. However, at the instigation of the shah of Iran, the Central Intelligence Agency (CIA, the U.S. government agency that conducts most international covert activities), and Israel, the Kurds rejected

Saddam meets with the shah of Iran (left) and Algerian president Houari Boumedienne in Algiers in 1975. That year, Saddam and the shah signed the Algiers Accord, agreeing not to interfere in their respective countries' internal affairs.

the terms and unleashed a bloody civil war. Within a year there were 60,000 casualties, among them 16,000 Iraqi soldiers.

It was only after Iraq agreed to the terms of the Algiers Accord in 1975, signed by Saddam and the shah, that the civil war came to an end. In the agreement, both countries agreed to refrain from interfering in the internal affairs of the other. This meant that no more weapons could reach the Kurds through Iran. Iraq, however, was forced to give up sovereignty over the eastern half of the Shatt Al-Arab waterway. A new border was drawn along the thalweg, the deepest part of the river. Having to share control of its only remaining outlet to the sea, Iraq felt extremely vulnerable. Still, as a result of the Algiers Accord, Iraq entered a period of stability for the first time in 50 years. Kurdish leaders, however, fled, and plans for Kurdish autonomy were shelved.

Despite their friendship treaty with the Soviet Union and the presence of Communist party members in their cabinet, the Baathis remained wary of Communist opposition and were watchful of the army, traditionally a hotbed of communism in Iraq. Realizing that no party could hold power in Iraq without the support of the army, Saddam decided to transform the politics of the military. After 1975, only Baathis were admitted to the military academy, and non-Baathis already in the army were passed over for promotion.

The Baathi suspicions proved warranted: In 1978 it was discovered that the Communist party was plotting against the government and had been able to infiltrate the upper ranks of the army. The officers implicated were promptly arrested and executed, and there followed a wave of arrests and torture of civilian Communists. Because the Iraqis considered the plot a breach of the friendship treaty with the Soviet Union, there ensued a period of strained relations with the Soviets.

In 1977 the Arab world was set reeling again. This time it was not a war with Israel but a peaceful encounter in Jerusalem that stunned the Arabs. In December, Egypt's president, Anwar Sadat, Nasser's successor, arrived in Israel in what was made to appear as a surprise visit but in reality had been orchestrated by the United States. Sadat kissed former Israeli prime minister Golda Meir warmly on both cheeks and addressed the Israeli parliament, opening the door for negotiations over the return of the Sinai Peninsula. In the United States, the visit was hailed as a bold gesture by a courageous Egyptian president; in the Arab world, Sadat's visit was widely considered a sellout of the Palestinians and the larger Arab cause.

The Baathis, who had long before made a serious commitment to the Palestinians, saw this development as a betrayal instigated by U.S. secretary of state Henry Kissinger, who with his shuttle diplomacy had set the stage for Sadat's visit before resigning his post earlier that year. Egypt's economy was in shambles, and the Baathis believed that the United States secretly promised Egypt aid in exchange for a gesture of goodwill toward the Israelis. To

Syrian president Hafez Al-Assad speaks at a minisummit in Damascus, Syria, in September 1978. At the summit, Assad and other Arab leaders criticized Egyptian president Anwar Sadat for his willingness to negotiate separately with Israel, which they considered a sellout of the Palestinians.

offset the U.S. strategy, Saddam rallied the wealthy Gulf leaders around the idea of increasing their aid to Egypt so that Sadat could withdraw from the negotiations with Israel. He sent Sadat a message promising him $5 billion from Iraq, but his offer was declined.

By the summer of 1978, Al Bakr's health had deteriorated badly, and Saddam was in full command. When in September of that year Sadat and Begin met with U.S. president Jimmy Carter at Camp David, Maryland, and negotiated the draft accords, Saddam organized an Arab summit to be held in Baghdad in November. At the Baghdad Summit, the Arab leaders agreed that Sadat's willingness to deal separately with Israel was a betrayal of the Arab and the Palestinian cause. They moved to expel Egypt from the Arab League, which had been led by that country since the organization's creation. They also decided to move the league's headquarters from Egypt to Tunisia. Finally, economic sanctions were put into effect against Egypt, and all the Arab countries broke diplomatic ties with that country.

As a result of Sadat's trip to Israel, Syrian leader Hafez Al-Assad had proposed a union of the Iraqi and Syrian armies and a joint political council between the two countries. The idea of such a union was very exciting for most Syrians and Iraqis, but eventually disagreements between the Syrian and Iraqi Baath made it impossible for the two countries to unite.

Nevertheless, Saddam had high hopes that Syria would eventually overcome these differences with Iraq and join together, a move that he believed would make both countries stronger. More important, the union would give the Arabs more strength against Israel. In January, Saddam traveled to Damascus to meet with Assad. Saddam was eager to salvage the idea of an Iraqi-Syrian federation, but the most Assad would agree to was a meaningless, united political command for the two regions, not unity. Saddam felt betrayed, and the bitter feelings between the two leaders grew worse in the years to come.

*Saddam Hussein became Baath party leader and president of Iraq
when Al Bakr resigned on July 17, 1979, the 11th anniversary of the
Baathi revolution. Saddam's first act as president was to purge the
party of alleged traitors through public executions.*

5

صّدّام حسَـــين

Judges

ON JULY 17, 1979, the 11th anniversary of the Baathi revolution, Al Bakr turned over the presidency and the party leadership to Saddam Hussein. A few days earlier, when Al Bakr had announced his decision to retire at a meeting of the RCC, the secretary had objected so strenuously to Saddam's succeeding him that Saddam later called him in for questioning. The secretary confessed that he belonged to a subversive group, formed in 1975 and funded by Syria, that had been planning to overthrow the Iraqi government. An investigation ensued in which 5 out of 21 RCC members were implicated. Eventually 22 senior Baath party members were convicted of treason and executed.

A chilling decision was made that permanently marred Saddam's presidency. Since the traitors were all Baathis, it was decided that ordinary civilian party members should join in the execution. Hundreds of delegates representing every Baathi party branch in Iraq participated.

Observers claimed that the prisoners had been tortured to obtain their confessions.

In their zealous pursuit of a pure revolution, the Baathis had become as repressive as the regimes against which they had once fought. As international human rights groups increasingly accused Iraq of torture and summary executions, it became clear that the many years of being on a war footing had seriously undermined the party's democratic ideals. A permanent siege mentality, carried over from their time in the underground, had set in.

Still, Saddam and the Baathi leadership claimed that the arrests and executions were necessary to repel the forces of counterrevolution, particularly those exerted by Syria. Others believed, however, that the repression was unwarranted, claiming further that because of these excesses the Iraqi revolution had lost its moral authority.

Meanwhile, Iran, too, was in the throes of revolution. The previous year, while in exile in An Najaf, Iraq, the leader of Iran's Islamic revolution, Ayatollah Ruholla Khomeini, had made speeches denouncing the shah and his regime. He had sent cassette recordings of the speeches to Iran, where they were reproduced and passed around the mosques and the bazaars. Before long, the Iranian people rose up to oust the hated shah, and on February 2, 1979, Khomeini returned triumphantly to Teheran, establishing the Islamic Republic in Iran under his jurisdiction. This was the beginning, Khomeini believed, of a revolution that soon would extend from Iran to the Arabian Peninsula. He envisioned the Islamic Republic ultimately to include the holy Shiite cities in Iraq, Mecca and Medina in Saudi Arabia, and Jerusalem—in effect, the Muslim world from Morocco to Malaysia.

The Iranian revolution entered a new phase in November, when a group of armed Iranians, mostly student activists, occupied the U.S. embassy in Teheran, taking everyone hostage. Their main purpose was to protest the granting of temporary asylum to the shah by the United States. The students claimed that for decades the shah had pandered to U.S. business interests to augment his own power and wealth at the expense of the Iranian people—a crime for which they believed he should pay. Although the shah's regime had responded repeatedly to political opposition with violent repression that included countless and flagrant human rights abuses, the United States supported the shah and even helped train his military police. Then, when he was ousted, the shah, now suffering from cancer, was allowed into the United States to receive medical treatment. Outraged that the United States would harbor one whose hands were soaked with the Iranian people's blood, the group stormed the U.S. embassy.

Meanwhile, in an attempt to establish a dialogue with Iran, Saddam had invited the new Iranian prime minister, a political moderate, to come to Iraq on a state visit. But before the visit could take place, revolutionary fervor swept the prime minister out of office. It soon became clear that the Iranian revolution was taking a turn toward the extreme, and Saddam knew there was no longer any chance of bettering relations between Iran and Iraq.

Saddam proved to be correct, as Iraq's pro-Khomeini Al Dawa-Al Islam, or Call of Islam, party, based in the holy cities of Karbala and An Najaf, began to create unrest in Iraq. In Karbala, in late 1979, 2 Al Dawa members opened fire on a religious procession, killing 1 and wounding 16 of their fellow Shiites. Believing that the attack had been carried out by the government, the Shiite community was enraged.

Before the year ended, the Soviet Union took advantage of the turmoil in the Middle East and invaded Afghanistan. Saddam immediately condemned this as an imperialist intervention, and relations with the Soviet Union, already strained, became even worse. Both Soviet and U.S. fleets began to arrive in the region, and U.S. president Jimmy Carter's government defined the Persian Gulf as a strategic American interest, warning that the United States would use military force to protect the oil for the West. In the Pentagon, plans were developed for a force capable of responding quickly to any emergency in the Gulf.

One such plan called for the introduction of U.S. troops into Iran, just north of the oil fields, in the face of a Soviet threat. But there was a hitch. To be feasible, a permanent U.S. military presence in the Gulf was needed, including sizable land bases. Otherwise, it would take several months to move American troops into place. But where? Israel was too far away, and besides, Arab states would protest. The island of Bahrain, off the Saudi coast, where the United States already had naval base rights, was too small. Kuwait, separated from Iran by only a short distance on the coast, was not much bigger. Iraq, moreover, had never relinquished its claim to Kuwait. Saudi Arabia, however, was both large enough, with a long coast on the Gulf as well as on the Red Sea, and was separated from Iran only by a short coastline. It shared a border some 500 miles long with Iraq as well, should trouble come from that direction. Most important, the Saudi regime was pro-U.S. But the Saudis flatly turned down the idea. In the end, the U.S. Rapid Deployment Force was based in Florida.

Meanwhile, Saddam was moving ahead with plans to modernize Iraq and turn it into a model society. In a region that was rife with government corruption, Saddam had decided that he would eradicate it from his own country. In his mind, corruption was not just morally wrong, it was high treason. In January, four government officials were executed for accepting bribes.

While vice-president, Saddam had continued the tradition of the early Muslim leaders, who made a practice of leaving their magnificent palaces disguised as ordinary people, sometimes even as beggars, to learn what the public sentiment was. Now, President Saddam Hussein also began a series of televised visits to every neighborhood and every village. One day he would turn up suddenly at an ancient Christian monastery, extolling the importance of the role of the Christians in fighting the Iranians (then the Persians); on another day, he would visit Kurdish peasants in their homes, inspecting their sanitary and refrigeration facilities, perhaps poking a piece of meat to see if it was fresh. Before long, it was understood that the president could drop in anywhere at any moment.

That year, UNESCO awarded Iraq a prize for its literacy program. When Saddam had launched it the year before, most of the population had been illiterate. At first, the religious communities and many of the traditionalists in the villages resisted having women taught to read and write. But there was imprisonment of one week for those who refused to enroll or allow a family member to do so, and absences brought fines. The state decreed that only those who could read and write would be able to get bank loans or new jobs, or even raises. In three years, illiteracy was practically eradicated in Iraq.

Saddam addresses the Iraqi Federation of Women in 1980. That year, the first parliamentary elections in Iraq in more than 20 years were held, and Iraqi women were given the vote for the first time. Progressive on women's issues, Saddam encouraged women to run for office.

Saddam had a special place in the hearts of Baathi women. Iraqi women had long enjoyed more freedom than did women in neighboring countries, and now he fully supported their continuing emancipation in the rural and religious communities, where a woman's role traditionally was restricted to bearing children and looking after the house. In 1978, a women's magazine was responsible for publishing the first photographs of Saddam with his wife and children at home. Until then, like all Arab men, he had kept a strict separation between his public and private life. His wife continued to work as a schoolteacher, and she began to appear in public sometimes, a strong break with tradition. The first parliamentary election in more than 20 years was held in 1980, and women were given the vote for the first time and encouraged to run for office, winning 7 percent of the seats.

Saddam was proud of Iraq's heritage and considered the fostering of culture an important government function. As president, he instituted prizes and gold medals for excellence in science, and he made huge allocations for archaeological excavations and for the restoration of historical sites. He created a budget for music and arts festivals, bringing artists from abroad to stimulate Baghdad's cultural life. He also built museums and commissioned paintings and sculptures for public places, saying he wanted to turn Baghdad into a garden of sculptures.

Meanwhile, the new president had not forgotten about Israel and the need to continue the fight for Arab rights in Palestine. On February 8, 1980, at a military ceremony, he proposed a national charter for the Arab states, meant to safeguard the 1978 Baghdad Summit gains and to foil the attempts to divide the Arabs.

The National Charter called for a rejection of all foreign forces and bases on Arab soil and for joint Arab military action to protect the regional sovereignty of any one state from aggression by a foreign power, including safeguarding Palestinian rights. The charter also called for a series of joint political and economic cooperative efforts aimed at Arab unity. Unlike the Arab League charter, it was binding and called for sanctions to enforce compliance. At a Baath party congress to discuss the charter, the official slogan was, "No military alliances, no foreign bases. All Arab forces for the liberation of Palestine." Saddam stated furthermore that the Americans were the enemies of the Arab nation because they used Israel as a weapon to prevent Arab unity. "The United States is occupying our lands through the Zionist entity," he said. "Israel occupies Palestine thanks to the strength of the United States."

In early March, Saddam explained prophetically, "We cannot imagine that the Jews would fear the hungry and the culturally, scientifically, and technologically back- ward. Israel does not fear the present Arab armies, which are 3 million strong. But it would fear an Arab army of half a million which was backed by a strong economy and an integrated community that was scientifically and technologically advanced." At another gathering, Saddam said, "Every stone laid in Iraq, all Iraqi training to use weapons, every scientist studying how to lay strong and firm foundations for Iraq—all these have as their central aim the liberation of Palestine. If Palestine is liberated, Arabs everywhere will be free." Soon, 12 Arab states and the Palestine Liberation Organization (PLO, the most prominent group dedicated to securing the rights of Pales- tinians and the establishment of a Palestinian state) had agreed to hold a summit to adopt the charter.

In Israel, Saddam's announcement of the National Charter caused shock waves. The Israelis immediately be- gan to make efforts to get a U.S. commitment for weapons and spare parts for Khomeini's army, which had inherited an American military infrastructure. The United States had imposed a trade embargo on Iran after the storming of the embassy, making the shipping of weapons from the United States to Iran illegal. Israel claimed to have intel- ligence that Saddam was preparing to take over the Iranian

The Ayatollah Khomeini, leader of the Iranian Islamic revolution, relaxes at his home-in-exile outside Paris, France, where he took up residence in October 1978. While in exile, Khomeini regularly exchanged insults with Saddam as tensions mounted between the two leaders.

oil fields. Therefore, they argued, in order to maintain the balance of power in the region, Iran needed to be supplied with weapons.

Israel had managed to maintain its ties with the Iranian government under the Khomeini regime. When they had seen the shah's rule weakening, the Israelis had immediately begun to cultivate relations with the Shiite religious community through Iranian Jews. During the shah's rule, in line with Israel's policy of forging ties with non-Arab Muslims, Israel had trained Iran's secret service and had persuaded Iran to invest in joint defense projects. Although Khomeini had broken relations with Israel and had pledged to restore Jerusalem to the Muslims and Palestine to the Palestinians, Iran remained a partner of Israel in the defense industry, and many of the same Iranian intelligence and military people were carried over. Now it became evident to Iran that the way to get more weapons and spare parts was through Israel.

In the spring, Iraq grew concerned as Khomeini increasingly spoke of exporting the Iranian revolution. There were public statements that Iran was planning to "liberate" the holy cities in Iraq and in Saudi Arabia. On a March 15, 1980, radio broadcast, Khomeini called on the Iraqis to rise up against Saddam. Then, Khomeini publicly claimed Bahrain, Kuwait, and southern Iraq as part of the Islamic Republic. Soon, the sons of the now-deceased Iraqi Kurdish leader, Mustafa Barzani, were invited to come to Teheran. Once again, Iran began providing the Kurds with weapons to destabilize Iraq. It also became apparent that Khomeini was pouring money into the Al Dawa party.

A turning point came on April 1, when a member of the Al Dawa party attempted to assassinate Tariq Aziz, Saddam's deputy prime minister. When Aziz began his speech at the Mustansiriyya University in Baghdad, a bomb was thrown at the podium. Aziz managed to get to the ground before it exploded, escaping injury. But a number of students were killed and injured. The police immediately arrested the Al Dawa party's number-two man, a mullah (a clerical official trained in doctrine and law) named Mohammed Bakr Sadr. The following day, Saddam turned up at the site of the assassination attempt in the pouring rain, drawing crowds of angry students around him. In a passionate speech, the rain pouring down his face, he vowed, "By God, the innocent blood that was shed at Mustansiriyya will not go unavenged."

On April 5, Al Dawa struck again. This time a bomb was thrown from an Iranian religious school into the funeral cortege of the students killed in the university attempt. More students were killed and injured. Bakr Sadr was executed along with several family members, and some 30,000 Shiites presumed to be of Iranian descent living in the holy cities were expelled from Iraq. This created a great deal of hostility because many Iraqi Arabs were included in the roundup. Very soon, there was an attempt on the minister of information's life. A close companion of Saddam's during the days of the underground, he pulled his pistol and personally chased the culprit down the street running at the head of his security detail. There were rumors that there was also an attempt on Saddam's life.

In a speech on the day of the funeral procession bombing, Saddam made it clear that he had lost all patience with the Iranian revolution. He spoke of a conflict "between the Arabs and the Persians" and called Khomeini a "shah in a turban." He said the Persians, or Iranians, were full of feelings of vengeance because they had once been conquered by the Arabs and had been converted to Islam by force, and now they wanted to turn Islam against the Arabs. He offered to assist Iranians in getting rid of Khomeini, and he called on Iran to return the three Gulf islands to the Arabs. He added that Iraq had agreed to the Algiers Accord (which called for mediation in the event of a border violation by either nation) under duress and called for a return to the pre-1975 boundaries of the Shatt Al-Arab. Then he demanded that Iran recognize the national rights of Arabs in Khuzistan, Iran's southwestern province, which the Ottomans had ceded to Persia in the mid-19th century.

After this, Khomeini and Saddam regularly exchanged public insults. Before the month was over, Khomeini declared that the Iraqi regime was attacking the Koran and Islam, a serious charge by a Shiite religious leader. In Iraq, more than half the population was Shiite and largely religious. Khomeini began calling openly over the radio for the Iraqi army to "overthrow Saddam as we did the shah."

In late April, the United States attempted to rescue the American hostages in Iran. The rescue attempt had to be called off, however, when the mission's helicopters began breaking down and running into each other in the desert. The debacle became a liability for U.S. president Carter, who had orchestrated the effort from the White House and would be running for reelection in November.

Although the United States, or the "Great Satan," as it was called in Iran, was the immediate object of Khomeini's ridicule after the failed rescue attempt, Iran's more immediate enemy, Saddam, was not forgotten. By now, Iraqi diplomats in Teheran were regularly harassed by Iranian religious authorities, and some of them had been injured in an attack. Two days after the rescue attempt, a report was leaked to the press in Teheran that there had been a coup in Iraq and that Saddam had been killed. Any hope the Iranians may have had that this news would precipitate a revolt was dashed, however, when Saddam appeared on Iraqi television that evening, calmly hosting a foreign dignitary.

While hostilities between Iraq and Iran intensified, Saddam continued to pursue his varied agenda. He proceeded with his development projects, which were quickly transforming Baghdad into a modern metropolis. The deadline set for the completion of some of these projects was 1982, when Saddam would be hosting a conference of the nonaligned countries (nations from around the world that had declared themselves politically independent from both the United States and what was then the Soviet Union, forming the Nonaligned Movement). He had been elected the next chairman of the movement at the organization's previous conference in Havana, Cuba. Saddam also continued laying the groundwork for the National Charter, to be signed by Arab nations, and planned to present a similar proposal to the nonaligned countries in 1982. His goal was to create a unified body of Third World countries that would stand up to the two superpowers.

Israel felt increasingly threatened as Saddam made strides toward creating not only Arab but even broader unified opposition to Israel and its sponsors. This was especially true because Israel knew it could no longer rely on the United States for unqualified support. During the Camp David negotiations between Egypt and Israel, Jimmy Carter had

U.S. president Jimmy Carter, Egyptian president Sadat (left), and Israeli president Begin (right) celebrate the signing of the Camp David peace treaty on March 26, 1979. Toward the end of his term, Carter became increasingly interested in the plight of the Palestinians.

shown a sincere interest in the plight of the Palestinians and was pressing Israel to relinquish the West Bank. In exchange for peace with Egypt, Israel was for the second time being forced to return the Sinai Peninsula, along with its oil wells, and was determined not to give up any more territory.

It was clear that a war between Iraq and Iran would help solve Israel's immediate problems. Such a war would divert attention from the Palestinian question and also interfere with the signing of Saddam's National Charter. But Israel also knew that Iran needed weapons, ammunition, and spare parts for its military.

There are many theories about U.S. involvement in arming Iran against Iraq. In his book *October Surprise* the former Carter administration official Gary Sick concluded that the promise of arms to Iran was made for political ends during the U.S. presidential election of 1980. In a 1991 PBS television documentary entitled "The Election Held Hostage," it was reported that Israel facilitated a secret meeting between U.S. presidential hopeful Ronald Reagan's campaign manager, William Casey, and a senior Iranian official. Sick writes that Casey and the Iranian met in Madrid, Spain, in July 1980 and discussed a promise of U.S. weapons and other military equipment to be delivered to Iran by Israel. In exchange, Iran would promise not to release the 52 American hostages it held until after the U.S. presidential elections in November, making a Reagan victory a virtual certainty. United States congressional hearings on this affair were pending in early 1992.

That summer, Iranian troops began to mass on Iraq's eastern border, and Iranian planes regularly violated Iraqi airspace. It became clear to Saddam that Iran was getting ready to march on Iraq. In August, he traveled to Saudi Arabia to meet with King Khalid, who was an important gauge of American reaction. It was well known that, despite their reluctance to allow U.S. military bases, the Saudis never made any important foreign policy decisions without first consulting the United States. Khalid agreed with Saddam that, in the event of war, Iraq would be fighting Iran on behalf of all the Arab states in the Gulf. The king urged Saddam to attack Iran if Iranian belligerence continued, and there was a promise that the most threatened Gulf states, namely Kuwait and Saudi Arabia, would help with the costs.

On September 4, 1980, Iran began shelling Iraqi towns and refineries along the border. Khomeini closed down the Shatt Al-Arab waterway and called over the radio to the mostly-Shiite inhabitants of Basra, Iraq's principal port city, to welcome him as a liberator. The Iran-Iraq war had begun.

It was Saddam's appraisal that although the Iranian army was three times the size of Iraq's, it was poorly organized after the shah's flight, and morale was low. Also, their equipment was in poor condition as a result of the impossibility of obtaining spare parts from the United States. Saddam calculated, therefore, that it would be possible to defeat the Iranian army within a few weeks.

On September 17, Saddam addressed the new Iraqi parliament. In view of Iran's repeated violations of the Algiers

Members of an Iraqi tank crew scramble during an Iranian air attack. When Iran began shelling Iraq on September 4, 1980, it began a war that would last eight years, drain both countries of valuable economic resources, and cost the lives of more than 600,000 people.

Accord, Saddam announced, Iraq considered the agreement null and void. Five days later, the Iraqi infantry marched onto the plains of Khuzistan while Iraqi planes bombed Iranian military installations. In less than a week, the Iraqis occupied a 45-mile-wide belt of land, and Saddam called for a cease-fire and the start of negotiations. But the war would not end so quickly; Israel had a great deal invested in its continuation and, following the election of President Ronald Reagan, the United States would join in this policy.

A bullet-riddled portrait of the Ayatollah Khomeini looms behind a group of jubilant Iraqi soldiers as they celebrate the retaking of the Fao Peninsula in April 1988. The territory had been in Iranian hands since February 1986.

6

صّدام حسّين

Lamentations

IRAN REJECTED THE IRAQI CEASE-FIRE PROPOSAL and continued the relentless bombing of Baghdad and Iraq's oil fields. Not only did the Iranian army not fall apart, as Saddam had expected it to, but with the help of the United States and Israel it managed to whip itself into fighting shape in a few months. Neither did an Arab uprising in Khuzistan materialize as the Iraqis had expected. Consequently, it became apparent to Saddam that the war with Iran would not end quickly.

Meanwhile, the United States continued to negotiate for the release of the hostages in Iran. Not wanting the hostage crisis hanging over his head on Election Day in November, President Jimmy Carter began to plan a second hostage rescue in the event negotiations failed. He had every reason to believe that he was close to getting the hostages released before Election Day. The hostages had been held captive for nearly a year, and everyone agreed that the Iranians had nothing more to gain by keeping them. Moreover, with the release of the hostages, more normal relations could resume between Iran and the international community, enabling Iran to trade more easily with the West, which it needed to do in order to continue the war with Iraq. Carter had received assurances that the Iranian parliament would vote for the hostages' release in October in exchange for the release of Iranian assets frozen in the United States. However, the Iranian parliament adjourned two days before the election, without ever having brought the matter of the hostages to the floor, and with the weight of the hostage crisis still hanging around his neck on Election Day, Carter failed to gain reelection.

Most Arab leaders, including Saddam, sighed with relief when in November 1980 Ronald Reagan was elected president and George Bush vice-president of the United States. Arabs had always been wary of the Democratic party because it was the party most identified with the pro-Israel lobby. Also, during the early 1970s, Bush had been the U.S. ambassador to the UN, where many high Arab officials had come to know him and believe he was their friend. Therefore, Arab leaders expected that Bush's presence in the Reagan administration would ensure that it would be sensitive to their needs.

While the Reagan-Bush ticket was celebrating victory, Israel was taking military action against Iraq. For some time, Israel and the West had been concerned about Iraq developing nuclear weapons and had taken measures to thwart the possibility. Earlier that year, for example, the Israelis had blown up a nuclear reactor core bound for Iraq before it could be shipped from La Seyne-sur-Mer, France, near Toulon. Also, that summer the Mossad, Israel's intelligence agency, had killed an Egyptian nuclear scientist working for Iraq in Paris. This time, on November 30, nearly three months into the Iran-Iraq war, the Israeli air force attempted to bomb an Iraqi nuclear reactor. This attempt failed, but later, in 1981, Israel was successful in destroying the Iraqi reactor complex outside Baghdad.

Still, the war with Iran raged on, and Saddam often went to the front himself to help direct assaults. It helped keep morale up in a war that showed no signs of ending. The Iraqi leader discussed problems with the soldiers and shared their meals. On one such visit to the front in March 1981, Saddam was almost captured by Iranian troops when they circled around the rear of the camp, cutting off his convoy, but his men were able to fight back the Iranians. Saddam continued to visit the front regularly.

By the spring of 1982, the war was going very badly for the Iraqis. Their supply lines were stretched thin, and Iran had begun to use human-wave tactics, sending thousands of untrained, lightly-armed adolescents and old men against Iraqi troops, attempting to overcome the Iraqis with the sheer number of Iranians on the battlefield.

In May, the Iraqis were pushed all the way back to the border, and Khomeini made Saddam's ouster a condition for stopping the war. Syria shut down Iraq's oil pipeline, leaving only the outlet through Turkey, which carried a mere 10 percent of Iraq's oil. (Assad and Saddam had become bitter rivals after the failed attempt to unify Syria and Iraq, and, furthermore, Assad belonged to a small Shiite sect, the Alawites, which had an affinity with Iran's Islamic revolution.) All other oil shipments had been stopped by Iran's bombing in the south. The war was costing Iraq more than $1 billion a month, and reserves, which had been $35 billion at the beginning of the war, were nearly depleted. Saddam's ambitious development program, which had continued on schedule, was cut back, and the summit of non-aligned countries was canceled indefinitely.

The Gulf states had already contributed $10 billion, and now they extended interest-free loans and grants of $25 billion to support Iraq's war effort. Saudi Arabia and Kuwait began to pump 300,000 barrels of oil a day for Iraq's account, to make up for Iraq's losses. They had either to help Iraq turn back the Iranians or to face the Iranians on Kuwaiti and Saudi soil.

In June 1982, at the same time that Iran was turning the tide of the war against Iraq, Israel invaded Lebanon. In September, the PLO was forced out of Beirut, and PLO leader Yasir Arafat moved his headquarters to Tunis, far away from Israel and Palestine. Unofficially, though, he moved his headquarters to Baghdad. After he left, with the Israeli Army standing watch, several hundred Palestinians were massacred in Beirut by the Israeli-supported Christian militia.

Close to desperation, with the Arab nation being attacked on two fronts (in Iraq and Lebanon) and his supply lines in Iran stretched thin, Saddam ordered a complete pullback of his troops in Iran to the Iraqi border, announcing a unilateral cease-fire. He then called a special meeting of the Baath party, and the party line was redefined. For the first time the Palestinian question was not touched on, and Iraqi nationalism was given precedence over Arab nationalism.

On July 14, the Iranians marched across the border into Iraq. The Iraqi lines held fast, however. In the fall, Iraq experienced shortages of goods and serious inflation, and Saddam was forced to introduce an austerity program. Nevertheless, the Iraqis rallied around their leader. Even the extremely religious Shiite community, wary of being conquered by the Persians, gave their support to Saddam. Their sons made up more than half of the army. Sunni Muslims made up only 45 percent of the population, and only half of these were Arabs. In Iraq now, there were no more Shiites and Sunnis; there were only Iraqis. The war had served to forge strong national bonds.

In the spring of 1983, the White House reviewed U.S. policy on Iraq and determined that Iraq's collapse would seriously harm U.S. interests. Thus began the so-called tilt toward Iraq, with the United States both increasing trade credits to Iraq and purchases of Iraqi oil.

Iran, though, had already embarked on a new policy that eventually would result in a reversal of this U.S. policy of

Opposite:
Saddam attends an Arab summit in Amman, Jordan, in November 1987. Earlier that year, Iranian forces were able to penetrate four of Iraq's five defensive lines, coming within artillery range of Basra, Iraq's most important seaport.

supporting Iraq. By sponsoring the taking of American hostages in Lebanon and by drawing out the negotiations for their release, Iran was able to extract ever greater concessions from the United States in the form of military intelligence on Iraqi weapons and a policy of extreme indulgence toward Iran. Israel had been shipping weapons and spare parts to Iran since the start of the war, but it cut back on arms sales to Iran when Iran began to gain the upper hand in the war, and the Iranians were angry. They were also angry about the Israeli invasion of Lebanon. As a result, Iranian-supported Shiite fundamentalists took their first American hostage in Lebanon in 1982.

In the fall of 1983, Iranian-supported Lebanese Shiites carried out a suicide mission at the U.S. Marine Barracks in Beirut, killing 290 marines. (In their book *Dangerous Liaison: The Inside Story of the U.S.-Israeli Covert Relationship*, political journalists Andrew and Leslie Cockburn cite the claim of a former Mossad officer, Victor Ostrovsky, that Israel had advance knowledge of the attack and did not warn the United States.) There as peacekeeping

Saddam poses for a 1987 family portrait with his wife, Sajida, and their daughter Hala (seated). Others pictured are (from left, standing) Colonel Saddam Kamel and his wife, Saddam's daughter Rina; son Koussai and his wife, Lama; daughter Raghid and her husband, General Hussein Kamel; and son Uday.

forces since after the Israeli invasion, U.S. troops were quickly withdrawn from Lebanon, and the incident was seen throughout the region as a U.S. defeat. Although the United States had been officially neutral in the Iran-Iraq war, it now began to encourage more arms sales to Iraq. Hostage-taking in Beirut continued, with the CIA station chief being taken in the spring of 1984.

Early that year, the Iranians launched an especially fierce offensive in the southern marshlands, capturing the oil-laden Majnoon Islands just north of Basra. Iranian troops executed Iraqi prisoners by the hundreds. Then, when Iran managed to cut off the highway from Baghdad to Basra, Saddam used chemical weapons and quickly turned the Iranians back. It was the first time Saddam had used chemical weapons, in violation of the Geneva Conventions, and he was widely condemned for doing so. Soon, Iran used chemical weapons as well.

The United States watched in horror as Iran advanced, fearing that after Basra the Iranians would move into Kuwait and then Saudi Arabia. That would place 85 percent of the capitalist world's oil reserves in Iran's hands. In fact, Iran made it known that it had every intention of taking control of the oil, which it claimed rightfully belonged to the Muslims. The United States and Iraq restored diplomatic relations in November, and the CIA opened up an office in Baghdad. Whereas before, the United States had made U.S. intelligence on Iraqi troop movements available to Iran, now the United States also provided Iraq with satellite pictures of the border, showing Iranian troop movements.

Iran launched its most successful offensive against Iraq in February 1986. Within 24 hours, Iranian forces took the Fao Peninsula, south of Basra, stopping just short of Iraq's only military port, on the Kuwaiti border.

Saddam, like Yasir Arafat earlier, had begun to lower his expectations. He had reached the conclusion that peace would have to be made with Israel. Also, the Baathis had come to realize that their earlier dream of one unified Arab state was no longer possible. They were recasting their aspirations for unity of the Arab nation instead along the lines of the emerging European Community, with a common market and a collective security encompassing separate states. With this new vision of the future, in a little-known move, Saddam directed Iraqi diplomats to meet secretly with the Israelis to explore the possibility of formal Iraqi recognition of the Jewish state.

Israel, however, rebuffed Saddam's overture, and there remains much debate about its reasons for doing so. A sympathetic view is that Israel simply did not trust Saddam Hussein. However, critics of Israel assert that it was not prepared to relinquish its own image as a Jewish state besieged by hostile Arabs, wanting to push the Jews into the sea, because that would have resulted in a drastic reduction in the more than $3 billion-a-year U.S. aid package to Israel as well as in the private contributions made from abroad, which are predicated largely on Arab hostility.

After the fall of Fao, the Arab Gulf states, led by Saudi Arabia and Kuwait, decided on a tactic of flooding the oil market to bring down the price of oil. In this way, the Arabs planned to diminish Iran's oil revenues, making it impossible for Iran to sustain its failing economy and pay for the war. At the same time, Saddam began attacking Iranian oil installations and tankers in the Gulf, hoping to bring about greater international pressure for Iran to agree to a cease-fire. Iran immediately retaliated by attacking Iraqi oil tankers. Iran also began to attack Kuwaiti ports and tried to spark an uprising among the large Shiite community in Kuwait, calling for the overthrow of its Sunni rulers, the Al-Sabahs. Kuwait soon asked for American naval escorts to protect its ships.

Then, in November 1986, it was revealed that for more than a year the United States had been selling missiles to Iran through Israel in exchange for hostages held in Beirut and had been using some of the proceeds to fund the contras, the rebels seeking to overthrow the socialist regime in Nicaragua. This was done despite the repeatedly stated U.S. policy of stopping the sale of weapons to Iran. It was these missiles that had made it possible for Iran to take the Fao Peninsula. As the scandal unfolded in the media, it became clear that the Reagan administration had secretly contravened its own official policy and circumvented Congress. Although all the details of Iran-contra would never be known because William Casey, who ran the operation with the White House, died the day before he was to testify at the congressional hearings probing the affair, the extent of U.S. duplicity toward Iraq was well documented. Reagan sent Saddam effusive apologies, but U.S.-Iraqi relations soured.

Early 1987 saw the worst Iranian offensive yet, as the Iranians again used their U.S.-made missiles to penetrate four of Iraq's five defense lines, coming within artillery range of Basra. Iraqis fled their homes by the thousands. It took three months to avert the danger of an Iranian breakthrough to Basra.

Saddam redoubled his bombing of Iranian tankers and oil installations in the Gulf, determined to bring the war to an end by further depriving the Iranians of their oil revenues. During this campaign, 37 U.S. sailors were killed when the USS *Stark*, a U.S. Navy vessel in the Gulf, was hit by an Iraqi missile some 85 miles north of Bahrain on May 17. The United States protested but accepted an apology from Iraq, which claimed that the strike was a mistake.

Meanwhile, Iraq was nearly ready to return to exporting its full share of the OPEC quota. Iraq's oil pipeline through Turkey was being expanded, and another pipeline through Saudi Arabia was almost completed. Saddam was determined to end the war and resume his development program.

In July, after Kuwait threatened to turn to the Soviets for help, the U.S. Navy began escorting Kuwaiti ships through the Persian Gulf. Still, despite the dangers to the Arab interests in the Gulf, the United States had been unable to

Kurdish children recite their lessons at a school in northern Iraq. In March 1988, Iranian forces took the Kurdish town of Halabja after some of the fiercest fighting of the war. Evidence later revealed that hundreds of Iraqi Kurds had been the victims of cyanide gas poisoning.

Israeli soldiers round up and frisk Arab men against a wall in the Israeli-occupied Gaza Strip as local Arab children pass by on their way to school. Harassment is common-place in the Israeli-occupied territories, where Palestinian Arabs are less than second-class citizens.

achieve a defense treaty with any of these states, not even with Kuwait.

While the United States pressed for a UN-sponsored cease-fire in the Gulf, Iran renewed its attacks, and the war heated up again, this time in northern Iraq. In August, Iran began a major effort to capture Iraq's mountainous northeastern province and sever the oil pipeline running from Kirkuk through Turkey. Iraqi Kurds worked closely with Iran to accomplish this.

In March 1988, the Iranians managed to take the Iraqi Kurdish town of Halabja, near the border. Some of the fiercest fighting of the war ensued in Iraq's effort to retake it, and Halabja became the site of one of the greatest tragedies of the war. After the fighting stopped, with Iran still in possession of the town, the international press was invited in. Hundreds of people lay dead in the streets, many of them Kurdish women clutching their dead babies, their dark blue lips indicating that they were victims of cyanide gas.

The Iranians condemned Saddam for gassing his own people, and the Kurdish rebels quickly joined in the condemnation, but Saddam denied the charges. The Pentagon later issued a report that said that although both sides used chemical weapons at Halabja, each apparently believing they were targeting enemy positions, there was no evidence that it was the Iraqis who gassed the Kurds. In fact, Iraq was not believed to have cyanide gas, whereas it was known that Iran did. The mayor of Halabja also said he believed it was the Iranians who gassed the Kurds. Although the Pentagon's findings on the Halabja massacre were reported by the *Washington Post*, they went largely unnoticed by most Americans. Instead, most U.S. media used the Halabja incident as definite proof that Saddam was a mass murderer. Later, there was another incident in which the Kurds claimed that Saddam had used chemical weapons. A UN inspection team, however, found bad burns but no evidence of gas.

When Iraq was finally able to retake Fao that spring, Saddam knew that Iraq would not lose the war. However, Saddam felt that Iraq's Gulf allies were being far too complacent, satisfied to allow the war to continue because it was no longer a threat to them. Iraq's development program and the strides made toward the emancipation of women clearly threatened the status quo they wanted to maintain. Moreover, unlike Iraq, these Gulf states had substantial, diversified investments in Europe and the United States, and their non-oil-related profits increased as the war pushed the price of oil down, profits that more than offset their losses in oil revenues.

Then, on July 18, 1988, Khomeini suddenly agreed to a cease-fire, saying, to do so "was more lethal for me than poison." Iran had been noticeably demoralized after a U.S. battleship in the Gulf had shot down an Iranian passenger plane on July 3, killing 290 passengers, even though the United States claimed it was a mistake. The cease-fire was seen as a victory for Iraq because Saddam's ouster was no longer an Iranian condition for stopping the war. Some 120,000 Iraqis and a half million Iranians had died in the war; the people had witnessed enough bloodshed. For two weeks, Iraqis joyously celebrated the end of the war.

Israel was taken by surprise—thanks to what has since been called by the Israeli intelligence community Israel's greatest intelligence failure ever—when the war ended suddenly. It was now faced with an Arab adversary many times stronger than it had been before the war. The Iraqi army was 1 million strong, battle hardened, and had 500 planes, 5,500 tanks, chemical weapons, and long-range missiles. The Iraqi military was developing biological and nuclear weapons as well. Moreover, Iraq had an agreement with Jordan to come to its military defense and was about to sign a nonaggression treaty with Saudi Arabia. Worst of all for Israel, for the first time in modern history, an Arab army was victorious.

Saddam arrives in Cairo in November 1988 to meet with Egyptian president Hosni Mubarak, who succeeded Sadat in 1981. The purpose of their meeting was to discuss the Palestinian question, to which Saddam increasingly turned his attention after the war with Iran ended.

7

صّدام حُسيـن

Hebrews

NOW THAT THE WAR WITH IRAN WAS ENDED, Saddam again turned his attention to the Palestinian question. He believed that the discord between Israel and the Arab world over the plight of the Palestinians was at the center of virtually all conflicts in the Middle East.

In December 1987, when some young Palestinians began throwing rocks at Israeli soldiers stationed in the occupied territories, a movement was born. The Intifada, as it became known, grew and intensified, and the world watched as Palestinians, armed with no more than bottles and stones, were beaten, teargassed, and fired upon by Israeli soldiers. Many international human rights groups condemned Israel for its treatment of the Palestinians and for using excessive force to quell the uprising. The Intifada was partly financed by Iraq, which sent the PLO some $4 million a month.

Then, on November 15, 1988, the PLO declared a Palestinian state in the West Bank and Gaza and called for Israel to withdraw. The declara-

Palestinian leader Yasir Arafat speaks to reporters at a press conference in Amman, Jordan. Concerned about the mass migration of Soviet Jews to the Israeli-occupied territories, Arafat called for an emergency Arab League summit to be held in Baghdad on May 28, 1990.

tion was made at a conference in Algiers, where Palestinian leaders also formally recognized the state of Israel and denounced terrorism. The PLO finally had endorsed a two-state solution to the Israeli-Palestinian conflict.

The next day, 27 countries recognized the state of Palestine. On December 13, Arafat called on Israel to enter into talks with the PLO under the supervision of the UN to "forge peace." He had the total support of Saddam. Even the United States, which at first had tried to stop Arafat from speaking at the UN by denying him an entrance visa, endorsed the

PLO leader's call for peace. But the Israelis refused to talk to Arafat, and the Intifada continued.

Meanwhile, Iraq was struggling to recover from the war with Iran, which left the country with a $100 billion foreign debt. Saddam's development plans were at a standstill, and there were no jobs for the slowly demobilizing army. Saddam had promised the Iraqis a constitution and more democratic political processes, but in the National Assembly elections, the Baath party won only 40 percent of the seats, and the end of the session came without the promised constitution. There emerged a raging debate among the Baathis over whether more democracy or more stability should come first. The Baathis feared that democracy would bring with it an Iranian-style Islamic government.

But Israel made it impossible for Saddam to attend only to domestic matters. With the cold war ending and the Soviet Union lifting its travel restrictions, Soviet Jews were making their way to Israel, which did whatever it could to attract as

Soviet Jews, eager to emigrate, wave Israeli flags as they wait in line at the Israeli consulate in Moscow. When the Soviet government decided to allow Soviet Jews to leave the Soviet Union in 1989, the creation and expansion of Jewish settlements in the occupied territories increased suddenly and dramatically.

many of them as possible. Anticipating as many as 2 million Soviet immigrants during the coming 5 years, Israel was eager to settle as many Jews as possible in the occupied territories and had stepped up housing construction. This alarmed the Arabs, who believed this was a continuation of the Zionist campaign to expel the Palestinians from the West Bank and Gaza.

On February 23, 1990, at an Amman summit meeting of the leaders of Iraq, Egypt, Yemen, and Jordan, Saddam expressed his outrage over Israel's campaign to settle Soviet Jews in the occupied territories and the treatment of the Palestinians by the Israeli military. He also warned of the increasing role of the United States in the region. The United States was helping to finance the relocation of the Soviet Jews in Israel, and the U.S. Navy continued to maintain a strong presence in the Persian Gulf. Saddam warned that this would lead to U.S. control of Arab oil and urged Arabs to pull their investments out of the West to influence U.S. policy.

Saddam was very critical of Arabs who allowed the United States to make decisions for them, and this put serious strain on his relationship with Egypt's president, Hosni Mubarak, who had succeeded Sadat after he was assassinated in 1981 by pro-Khomeini extremists. During the Iran-Iraq war, Egypt had thrown its support behind Iraq, sending weapons and ammunition, as well as military advisers and pilots, and Saddam had led a campaign to readmit Egypt into the Arab League. But when Saddam appeared to criticize Mubarak's ties to the United States, the Egyptian president left the summit in a rage.

Before he left, Saddam chastised his Gulf allies in the war with Iran—Kuwait, Saudi Arabia, and the United Arab Emirates—for pressing him to repay the war debt. Saddam was proud of having been able to stymie Iran's efforts to export the Islamic Revolution to Iraq and the Arabian Peninsula, despite the setback this had meant for Iraq's own development plans. In Saddam's mind, Iraq had fought the war not only for its own interests but on behalf of all the countries in the Persian Gulf region. He reminded Arab leaders that it had been understood that all war debts incurred in the effort to keep Iran out of Arab territory—specifically the Arabian Peninsula—would be shared by all the Gulf states. It had been understood, Saddam said, that Iraq would not be expected to repay the loans, and certainly not in full.

Kuwait also appeared to have forgotten that the Arab leaders, along with flooding the oil market to lower prices and thereby sapping Iran's buying power, had agreed to make up the difference to Iraq, which was similarly affected by the drop in prices while fighting the war. Furthermore, after the end of the war, when Saddam had sought to renew the border talks with Kuwait, he found that the Kuwaiti government had moved the border north to encompass the southern tip of Iraq's Rumaila oil field and had extracted several billion dollars worth of Iraqi oil.

Moreover, on the very day after Iraq's cease-fire with Iran, Kuwait, in violation of its OPEC quota, had begun flooding the market with oil again. Kuwait was earning more than $6 billion a year from its investments overseas, which exceeded its oil revenues. By contrast, every dollar the price dropped cost Iraq $1 billion. Iraq's oil revenues, which made up 90 percent of its income, dropped to $7 billion a year—down from $30 billion in 1980—barely the amount of its debt service payments. There was not a penny left over, not even for Iraqi subsistence, let alone for renewing Saddam's development program. Iraq could not even pay for the food it imported.

After the Amman Summit, Kuwait and the United Arab Emirates had begun again to flood the oil market. Saddam did not doubt that there was a correlation between this betrayal and his speech at the summit, in which he warned of U.S. control of Arab oil.

On February 6, 1990, a Pentagon spokesman had briefly summarized the classified contents of the new U.S. Defense Policy Guideline for 1992–97. After the Soviet invasion of

Afghanistan in 1979, the Gulf oil had been declared vital to U.S. national security interests, and it had been decided to defend it militarily if necessary. Now, with the Soviets no longer seen as the main threat, the first line of defense had been moved from Iran. Still designed to defend the Western nations' main oil supply, the Pentagon defined the new mission as the defense of the Arabian Peninsula, possibly with an air attack, against regional threats. Since Iran was expected to remain deflated for some time, this new focus clearly meant Iraq.

The United States, however, still had no military bases in the area and no defense agreements with any of the Gulf countries. A large part of the reason for this had been the Baathis' objection to any foreign military forces on Arab soil during the past 20 years and Saddam's continuing appeals to Arab nationalism. The most the United States had been able to achieve was the secret building of runways and bunkers in the desert, mostly in Saudi Arabia. These installations, as well as many of the sophisticated weapons bought from the United States, were run largely by former American intelligence and military personnel, hired from the private sector by the Arabs but widely held to be working under Pentagon orders. However, there were still no U.S. ground forces in the area.

The strain in U.S.-Iraqi relations intensified when Farzad Bazoft, an Iranian-born journalist working for a British newspaper, was arrested in Baghdad on charges of espionage. After confessing that he was working for both British and Israeli intelligence, Bazoft was executed.

Although there was evidence that Bazoft had indeed been working as a spy, the execution was widely condemned in the West as the result of a confession obtained under torture. The *New York Times* columnist William Safire, for example, called the Bazoft execution a "state murder" and Saddam "the dictator of what has become the world's most dangerous nation." Safire speculated that an Iraqi military installation on which Bazoft had been seeking information was producing "poison gas, rockets, or nuclear weapons." Before long, both the *New York Times* and the *Washington Post* were calling for sanctions against Iraq.

In the spring of 1990, Saddam concluded that Israel was planning an air attack on Iraq's military installations. On April 2, he made an impassioned speech to the Iraqi army, warning that if Iraq was attacked it would respond militarily. Wearing a khaki uniform with a general's insignia on the shoulders, Saddam warned that if Britain and the United States thought that their criticism could provide cover for an Israeli attack on Iraq, they were mistaken, "because, by God, we will make the fire eat up half of Israel if it tries to do

At the Baghdad Summit, Saddam charged Kuwait with waging an "economic war" on Iraq. Iraqi foreign minister Tariq Aziz, pictured here, drafted the memorandum detailing Iraq's grievances against Kuwait and later played an important role in the effort to bring about a peaceful solution.

anything against Iraq." Iraq, he said, had an arsenal of advanced chemical weapons equal to the United States or the Soviet Union. "Whoever wants to occupy Iraq," he continued, "let him come forward. We are not carrying the banner of challenge, as we are not defying anyone. But if anyone challenges us, he will find us stronger than a diamond. . . . We will not be trampled upon."

In May, Yasir Arafat ordered several thousand PLO guerrillas to relocate in Iraq to stand against a possible Israeli attack. Indeed, according to Andrew and Leslie Cockburn, the attack was called off in June because the United States refused to give the green light. Arafat also called for an emergency Arab League summit to discuss the growing influx of Soviet Jews to Israel, warning that this could lead to war. A summit was scheduled for May 28 in Baghdad.

At the summit, Saddam complained bitterly to the other Arab leaders of the "economic warfare" being waged against Iraq by Kuwait and the United Arab Emirates. He noted that Kuwait's production above its OPEC quota in the two years since the end of the war with Iran was a deliberate assault on Iraq's economy that had cost Iraq some $28 billion, far more than the $17 billion Kuwait claimed to have loaned Iraq for the war. "We cannot tolerate this type of economic warfare," he said. "We have reached a state of affairs where we cannot take this pressure." He continued, "War does not mean just tanks, artillery, or ships. It can take subtler and more insidious forms, such as the over-production of oil, economic damage and pressures to enslave a nation."

At an OPEC meeting in early July, the Kuwaitis, under pressure from the Saudis, agreed to revert to their oil quota. But immediately after the meeting they announced that they planned to go back to overproduction within two months. On July 15, Iraq's foreign minister, Tariq Aziz, wrote a long memorandum to the Arab League outlining Iraq's griev- ances against Kuwait. The following day, Saddam, in his annual address to the nation, made it clear that he was planning to resort to military force against Kuwait if the problems were not solved. "If words fail to protect us, we will have no choice but to go into action to reestablish the correct state of affairs and restore our rights."

On July 18, Saddam began deploying 30,000 troops on the border, and the Arab leadership, seeing that Saddam meant business, began to urge Kuwait to settle its differences with Iraq. The United States reacted by putting its naval units on alert and conducting maneuvers in the Gulf.

Saddam saw the Kuwaiti aggression toward his country as part of the Zionist effort to undermine Iraq's plans for industrialization. The recent Baghdad summit and the increasing intensity of the Intifada had given new urgency to the question of Palestine. Palestinian protests had spread beyond the occupied territories into Israel proper, and clashes between protesters and Israeli soldiers had resulted in nearly 1,000 casualties. The international community became increasingly critical of Israel's use of what many viewed as excessive force, and Israel now looked to settle the Palestinian question. Israel stepped up its campaign to expel the Palestinians from Gaza and the West Bank and also sought to cut off the support that the Intifada was receiving from foreign sources. Saddam concluded that Israel's most immediate goal in settling the Palestinian question was the destruction of Iraq, a key provider of that support and a defender of Jordan if there was trouble on the border. He believed further that the administration of U.S. president George Bush had aligned itself with Iraq's enemies.

Israel was already the U.S. strategic ally in the region, and Saddam was convinced that, for all the talk in Washington, D.C., about maintaining the balance of power in the Middle East, there was a U.S. plan to tip the balance toward Israel. He believed that the United States wanted to make Israel the U.S. policeman in the Gulf, eventually using the Israeli military to watch over American oil interests.

Jaber Al-Ahmed Al-Sabah, the emir of Kuwait. Even as some 100,000 Iraqi troops amassed along the Kuwaiti border, the Kuwaitis were not eager to negotiate because they were confident that should Iraq attack, the United States would come to Kuwait's assistance.

On July 25, Saddam met with the U.S. ambassador to Iraq, April Glaspie, and laid out his points in much the same way that he had done previously at the Amman and Baghdad summits. The American ambassador replied clearly that the United States had "no opinion on Arab-Arab conflicts." Then, Saddam, in a reference to an upcoming meeting with the Kuwaitis, explained, "If, when we meet, we see that there is hope, nothing will happen. But if we are unable to find a solution, then it will be natural that Iraq will not accept death." A week later, Ambassador Glaspie left for Washington, D.C., a further indication to Saddam that the United States was not worried.

Saddam planned to meet with the Kuwaiti emir in Jidda, Saudi Arabia, on July 31 to negotiate. Saddam made it clear to Arab leaders that he would refrain from using force after this meeting only if after the negotiations there was hope for a peaceful solution. One of those leaders, King Hussein of Jordan, went to Kuwait on July 28 to convey the urgency of reaching a solution and Saddam's willingness to use force if the negotiations were not fruitful. However, the Kuwaiti foreign minister, the emir's brother, said he was confident that the United States would defend Kuwait and refused to negotiate. On the same day, at Saddam's request, Arafat flew to Kuwait with an offer of the continued use of the Rumaila oil field in exchange for $10 billion. But the emir refused to discuss the matter.

By the end of July, when Glaspie was meeting with Saddam, there were 100,000 Iraqi troops on the Kuwaiti border, and the CIA had already reported to the White House that the Iraqi deployment, given the nature and extent of the supply lines, could no longer be considered a simple exercise in intimidation. However, based on statements made by Deputy Secretary of State John Kelly at a congressional hearing on July 31, Saddam had no reason to believe that the United States would become involved militarily in the event of an Iraqi attack on Kuwait. Kelly said that the United States had no defense treaty with the Gulf states and called the question of whether the United States would come to the aid of Kuwait highly hypothetical. These statements were heard in Iraq over BBC Radio.

When at the last minute the emir announced that he would not attend the meeting but would send a representative, a furious Saddam also refused to attend. At the meeting, the Iraqis found that the Kuwaitis showed no disposition to settle their differences, and the talks quickly broke down.

Well before sunrise on the morning of August 2, 1990, Saddam, conducting the operation from the safety of his bunker deep below the Presidential Palace, ordered Iraqi troops into Kuwait.

U.S. fighting machinery arrives at a Saudi port in preparation for war with Iraq. The U.S. military plan was ostensibly one to defend Saudi Arabia from Iraqi aggression. However, it soon became clear that the Pentagon was moving swiftly and deliberately into an offensive mode.

8

صَدَّام حُسَين

Revelation

THE VERY DAY THAT SADDAM sent his troops into Kuwait, U.S. transport planes began taking off every few minutes for the Persian Gulf. The following day, reports came out of the Pentagon that Iraqi troops were being positioned a half mile from the Saudi border. Reports stated that 100,000 elite Iraqi troops were in the south of Kuwait, their weapons aimed at Saudi Arabia.

There is much controversy surrounding the events of the next few hours and days. Jordan's King Hussein claims that Bush had promised him that he could have until Saturday afternoon to secure a commitment from Saddam and had agreed not to pressure Arab leaders to condemn Iraq. But, on Friday morning, the U.S. State Department not only pressured Egypt but also urged the Soviets to condemn Iraq. That same day the United States and Britain began pressing for UN sanctions, including a trade embargo against Iraq, to force compliance with UN Resolution #660, which called for Iraq's withdrawal from Kuwait. The

Bush administration argued that the threat to Saudi Arabia was great and that protective measures had to be taken.

Although Mubarak had agreed to support efforts to negotiate a peaceful solution, under U.S. pressure he condemned the Iraqi invasion. His timing was especially bad because he issued his condemnation only shortly before Jordan's Hussein returned with a commitment from Saddam that he would withdraw immediately. In fact, Iraq had already announced on Baghdad Radio that it would begin pulling its troops out of Kuwait on Sunday.

Then, on Friday, August 3, Bush summoned the Saudi ambassador, Prince Bandar bin Sultan, to the White House. He was presented with satellite photographs that supposedly showed Iraqi troops dug in along the Saudi border in an offensive position. (In fact, the *St. Petersburg Times* obtained satellite pictures of the border reportedly taken a few days later that showed that the roads were covered with sand; there was no Iraqi military activity in the south.) The prince was then showed a plan for the U.S. defense of Saudi Arabia, which the United States had drawn up nearly nine years earlier. The U.S. government, he was told, was prepared to implement the plan immediately, with King Fahd's approval. After the meeting, Bandar called his uncle, the king, telling him about the satellite pictures and the U.S. plan. However, the king needed more convincing before he would allow U.S. troops on Saudi soil.

That evening, Bush called Fahd and urged him to go along with the plan, stressing the need for action to counter the Iraqi threat. Still, Fahd said he wanted to wait, that he had confidence in King Hussein's efforts to persuade Saddam to withdraw. Nevertheless, the following day, the king canceled the summit scheduled with Saddam.

The following morning, General H. Norman Schwarzkopf, who would command the allied ground forces during the war, explained in a briefing to Bush that the defense phase of the operation would take four months and a quarter million troops to complete. If it was then decided to go on

the offensive to force Iraq out of Kuwait, it would take another quarter million men and another four to eight months. Therefore, the United States could be ready to take military action somewhere between March and June.

Saddam believed that by taking the entire country of Kuwait he had made it impossible for U.S. troops to find a land base in the Gulf. He never believed that the Saudis would give the United States a base for a military operation, especially one against Iraq, in view of the nonaggression treaty between Iraq and Saudi Arabia. Still, on Sunday, August 5, Saddam ordered Iraqi troops to begin to withdraw from Kuwait. He also sent a message to the White House and to the Arab leaders, saying that he was ready to negotiate and giving assurances that he had no plan to invade Saudi Arabia.

Western leaders, however, in both Europe and the United States, insisted that the Iraqi leader was simply buying time

U.S. general H. Norman Schwarzkopf and Saudi king Fahd review U.S. troops in eastern Saudi Arabia on January 7, 1991. A great deal of effort on the part of the White House was necessary to persuade Fahd, who did not believe his country was threatened by Iraq, to allow U.S. troops to be deployed on Saudi soil.

to better position his troops for an invasion of Saudi Arabia. The United States set about forging an international fighting coalition as the crisis took center stage at the UN.

U.S. secretary of defense Richard Cheney traveled to Saudi Arabia on Sunday to get Fahd's approval of the U.S. defense plan. On the plane, he decided not to stress the importance of the satellite pictures because, he admitted, U.S. intelligence officers had no indication that Iraq would invade Saudi Arabia. Nevertheless, Cheney began his presentation, "Saudi Arabia faces what may be the greatest threat in its history." General Schwarzkopf, who had accompanied the defense secretary, added authoritatively, "Saddam could attack Saudi Arabia in as little as 48 hours."

Schwarzkopf proceeded to outline the U.S. plan in great detail, never saying, however, that this meant moving a quarter of a million U.S. troops to Saudi Arabia. When the Saudis said that a permanent U.S. military base in the kingdom was absolutely out of the question, Cheney promised that all U.S. troops would leave as soon as the job was done. When the briefing ended, Fahd gave his approval.

Fielding questions for television journalists that same day (August 5) Bush said, "I view very seriously our determination to reverse out this aggression. . . . This will not stand, this aggression against Kuwait," thereby committing the United States to a military offensive if Saddam did not withdraw. Thus, Bush had upgraded the U.S. military goal from defending Saudi Arabia to forcing Iraq out of Kuwait, and the chairman of the joint chiefs of staff, General Colin Powell, was astonished to hear the news for the first time as he watched television. Saddam immediately canceled the withdrawal of Iraqi troops from Kuwait, which had begun that day. The next afternoon, Bush gave the order for Operation Desert Shield to begin.

Saddam was furious. He had spent the morning of August 6 explaining to the U.S. chargé d'affaires in Baghdad that Iraq would not march on Saudi Arabia because it had no historical reason for doing so, which, he pointed out, was not the case with Kuwait. Now, faced with the threat of war, Saddam prohibited several thousand foreigners in Kuwait and Iraq, including 2,500 Americans, from leaving. A few days later, confident that the United States would not target locations where American civilians would be harmed, Saddam ordered that these so-called guests be rotated to Iraq's strategic sites.

Although this defense tactic was effective from Iraq's standpoint, by using civilians as human shields, Saddam was playing into the hands of his Western critics. The Western media promptly characterized Saddam as a violent radical, a hostage-taker, and a terrorist, and the American public responded by tying yellow ribbons everywhere, just as they had when the American hostages were held in Iran.

By August 8, only six days after the invasion of Kuwait, thousands of U.S. troops were taking positions in Saudi Arabia. In a televised press conference, Bush said, "A line has been drawn in the sand," and that evening, in an address to the nation, he compared Saddam to the World War II German dictator Adolf Hitler. He continued to state that the U.S. mission in the Gulf was strictly defensive while sanctions against Iraq were given a chance to work. Nevertheless, by the time he had ended his speech, asking the country to pray for peace, the U.S. president had cleared the way for war. That same day, Saddam announced Kuwait's annexation, making Kuwait Iraq's 19th province.

As it became more apparent that Iraq did not intend to attack Saudi Arabia, the defense of that country was no longer a plausible justification for the U.S. military presence there. So, during the following months, the Bush administration offered other reasons for the troop buildup, including the defense of Western oil interests, the destruction of Iraq's secret chemical and nuclear weapons capabilities, U.S. jobs, and, more generally, the creation of a "new world order."

Bush and his advisers understood that to garner support for a U.S. war with Iraq they had to rally the American public around a cause. But up to that point the attempts to justify the U.S. military action had met with mixed results. Even the noble-sounding ideal of a new world order seemed vague. So the administration compared Saddam with Hitler. Like Hitler, the argument went, Saddam planned to conquer his neighbors one by one in a quest for world domination. Saddam had gassed his own people, the Kurds, just as Hitler had gassed his, the Jews. U.S. officials maintained that it was impossible to negotiate with Saddam, who, like Hitler, was a liar and could not be trusted. Clearly, they said, force was the only language Saddam understood, and nothing less than his total humiliation would make the world safe for democracy.

At the UN, alliances formed quickly, as did the consensus for war. The United States forged an international coalition and pushed resolutions through the UN Security Council. Eventually, all of Europe, much of the Third World, and the Soviet Union, which received $1.5 billion from Saudi Arabia and promises of U.S. economic support, allied themselves with the United States against Iraq. Egypt was forgiven a $7 billion loan by the United States and received $5 billion from the Gulf states after Mubarak pushed the Arab League to condemn Iraq.

On the other side, there were those who opposed the use of force and favored negotiations to get Iraq out of Kuwait, but the United States was not kind to its detractors. For example, King Hussein, who supported negotiations with Saddam, was immediately discredited in the Western media, and although he supported UN sanctions and remained neutral, he was accused of, and condemned for, siding with Saddam. Also, Yemen, which voted with Cuba against the United States at the UN, was informed by a U.S. delegate, "That's the most expensive vote you've ever cast." Shortly thereafter, the United States canceled an $80 million aid package to Yemen.

Meanwhile, Israel was given another $1 billion of U.S. military aid in August, as well as $700 million to improve its antimissile system and a $400 million loan guarantee for housing for Soviet Jews. Many Americans objected to the size of this aid package, believing it inappropriate to send enormous sums of money abroad while an increasing number of people back home were jobless, homeless, and living below the poverty level. According to the U.S. Census Bureau, in 1990, some 34 million Americans were living in poverty, and this estimate was considered conservative. Moreover, many Americans had inadequate health care for themselves and their families, and education was in a state of crisis. Despite these objections, the United States later promised Israel an additional $10 billion in loan guarantees.

Faced with a U.S. ultimatum, Saddam believed he could no longer discuss a withdrawal from Kuwait without compromising his own stature as a leader. Consequently, he was forced to look for a way to withdraw from Kuwait that would enable him to save face. One way to do this, he believed, was to link a withdrawal from Kuwait to the Palestinian question, which in his mind was the root of all problems in the region.

At the UN on August 12, 1990, Saddam proposed a simultaneous withdrawal by all countries from all the occupied territories. Israel had ignored earlier UN resolutions calling for a withdrawal from the Israeli-occupied territories. Saddam's proposal included not only Israel's withdrawal from the territories it occupied but also Syria's withdrawal from Lebanon and Iraq's from Kuwait. Saddam believed his offer was a reasonable one, but it was derided by the White House and portrayed by the Western news media as a propaganda ploy.

In October, Bush ordered the doubling of the number of U.S. troops in the Gulf to a half-million, going from a defensive into an offensive mode. In early November, he made this decision public. Later that month, the UN Security Council passed Resolution #678, authorizing the use of military force if Iraq did not leave Kuwait by January 15, 1991.

After the UN vote, Bush proposed a meeting between himself and the Iraqi foreign minister, Tariq Aziz, and another between Saddam and U.S. secretary of state James Baker, to be held before the January 15 deadline. Bush quickly added, however, that the U.S. position had not changed and was not negotiable: Iraq must withdraw from Kuwait unconditionally by the deadline, or else. Because Saddam would not withdraw unconditionally and Bush would not consider a conditional withdrawal, there was no basis for negotiation, and the proposed meetings never took place. As a goodwill gesture, however, Saddam ordered the release of all the foreigners being held in Iraq.

In early December, Algeria made a serious effort to mediate negotiations with Iraq. King Hussein also continued his effort to bring about a peaceful resolution to the conflict. But Bush stood firm: He would accept nothing less than an unconditional Iraqi withdrawal. "Your country treats me with the condescension of a colonial power toward a colony," Saddam earlier told the American civil rights leader and politician Jesse Jackson. The choice of either fighting or surrendering, Saddam said on several occasions, was no choice at all: He had to fight.

Despite the U.S. troop buildup and tough talk from Bush, Saddam and his inner circle remained unconvinced that the United States would actually go to war over Kuwait. Recalling the power of protest in the United States during the Vietnam War, the Iraqis reasoned that the antiwar movement in the United States would carry the day. Also, many U.S. congressional leaders had expressed strong opposition to the use of force in the Gulf. At most, the Iraqis believed that the United States planned a limited war.

On January 9, 1991, Tariq Aziz and James Baker met in Geneva, Switzerland. In what was the first high-level meeting between Iraq and the United States since the beginning of the crisis, Aziz and Baker met for more than six hours. The Iraqis asked for only one thing: that the United States withdraw its ultimatum and retract the January 15 deadline.

They believed that a peaceful solution could be reached if time were allowed for negotiations. But the United States said the deadline stood firm. When Baker emerged from the meeting, he simply said that he had once again delivered Bush's ultimatum to Iraq. Tariq Aziz, in his press conference following the meeting, appealed for a solution that addressed the Palestinian question.

On Capitol Hill, members of Congress took to the podium one after the other to argue for or against the use of force in the Gulf. Some believed the United States was right to go to war, many felt the pressure of the pro-Israel lobby, which advocated war, others listened to the wisdom of men and women all across the United States whose sons and daughters were stationed in the Gulf, still others simply believed it wrong to go to war as long as a peaceful solution was even remotely still possible. But in the end, the speeches mattered very little: On January 12, the U.S. Senate voted by a margin of 52 to 47 to approve the use of military force.

Six of the senators who voted affirmatively cited as a reason that Iraqi soldiers had killed babies at a Kuwaiti hospital by removing them from their incubators. However, after the war it was dicovered that the story was part of a Kuwaiti public relations campaign and completely untrue.

During the second week of August an organization called Citizens for a Free Kuwait, heavily funded by the Kuwaiti government, had hired a public relations firm to shape American public opinion in favor of U.S. military action against Iraq. The firm, run by a former chief of staff to vice-president Bush, arranged for hearings on supposed Iraqi atrocities before the U.S. Congress and the UN. At those hearings, a Kuwaiti doctor and a 15-year-old girl stated that they had witnessed Iraqi soldiers take babies from their incubators and leave them on the floor to die. The doctor said further that he had buried some of the dead babies himself. The international human rights group Amnesty International included this testimony in a report; an outraged

George Bush cited the story publicly numerous times during the fall, and the American public was appalled at the Iraqi barbarians. After the war, however, it was revealed that the doctor was actually a dentist, that the girl was the Kuwaiti ambassador's daughter. Amnesty International retracted its endorsement of the story. For the first time, the services of a professional public relations firm had been engaged in the manipulation of the public to commit the United States to a full-scale war.

Meanwhile, General Norman Schwarzkopf had been under great pressure to complete the preparations for an offensive by the January 15 deadline, despite his having told the president that he could be ready by March at the earliest. During the last week of December, Schwarzkopf secretly

The U.S. battleship Missouri *fires on Iraqi targets on January 17, 1991, the first day of Operation Desert Storm. At first, the United States and its allies flew 2,000 air sorties a day over Baghdad; after a few weeks, some 3,000 were flown each day. Iraqi defenses were ineffective.*

received the order from the president to begin the attack on January 17 at 2:00 A.M., local time.

Desert Storm began on schedule. By 2:30 A.M., allied bombers were pounding Baghdad. There were between 2,000 and 3,000 air sorties each day. The Iraqi defense systems proved ineffectual from the start. By the second day, Iraq's electrical power stations were destroyed, leaving the Iraqi civilian population without electricity for the duration of the war. Thus, there was no elevator service, no water purification, no bathrooms, no television, and no refrigeration. In addition, the sewerage system did not function, and water often could not be boiled. The stores of meat and fresh produce throughout the country quickly spoiled. In the hospitals, medicines went bad, and doctors were no longer able to sterilize their equipment. Incubators ceased to function. The mail service outside the country had already been halted under the UN embargo, so when the country's telephone facilities were bombed, it became impossible for most Iraqis to communicate their plight to the outside world.

Each afternoon during the war, the Pentagon held a press conference in which high-ranking officials would answer questions, point at maps, and show videotapes. The abstract quality of the videotapes made the war seem like a computer war game in which there were planes dropping bombs on buildings, bridges, and roads without any effect on civilians. To reinforce this portrayal of the bombing, the Pentagon emphasized that the strikes on Baghdad were surgical and proceeded to show footage of so-called smart, or super-accurate, bombs being directed by U.S. pilots with remarkable precision. The Western news media ran very little footage showing the plight of the Iraqi people, while it repeatedly aired the aerial footage made available by the Pentagon. Later, the Pentagon estimated that only 7 percent of the bombs used by the United States and its allies during the war were of the smart variety and that nearly 80 percent of the regular bombs missed their targets, causing considerable damage to civilian property.

A Baghdad woman walks amid the destruction wreaked on the city by allied bombing. Throughout the war, U.S. president Bush insisted that the United States had no dispute with the Iraqi people but only with Saddam; however, the Iraqi people, not Saddam, were the ones to suffer the hardship and loss of life.

Arab women shout anti-U.S. slogans and carry placards at a pro-Iraq demonstration in Amman, Jordan, on January 14, 1991. The placard bearing a picture of the Iraqi leader also bears a caption, which reads, The Hero of Liberation, the Maker of Peace and Victory, Historical Leader Saddam Hussein.

At one point, the Iraqis opened a number of oil pipelines in an attempt to clog Saudi Arabia's water purification system and set the Gulf waters on fire. As oil poured into the Gulf, the Western media featured pictures of oil-covered birds dying on the beaches, prompting an outcry from environmentalists. Arabs noted bitterly that Westerners seemed to care more about those birds than about the people being slaughtered on a daily basis by U.S. bombers in Iraq.

Several weeks into the heavy bombing, the Soviets made a highly publicized attempt to negotiate a solution, Iraq's foreign minister, Tariq Aziz, traveled back and forth to

Moscow. For a few days, hopes ran high for a negotiated end to the fighting, but this failed to materialize.

The effect of this failed attempt to end the war was devastating for the Iraqi forces. From the beginning, Saddam had feared that if he showed a willingness to negotiate, the army would lose its will to fight. Now, just as he had anticipated, the already beleaguered Iraqi soldiers' high hopes for peace were dashed by the political reality of the U.S. insistence on an unconditional withdrawal from Kuwait, and Iraqi soldiers began to surrender by the thousands. They had been under U.S. bombardment around the clock for more than a month and had little or no food and water left. Also, communications between the front lines and the Iraqi military command had largely been cut.

On February 25 in Iraq, one day after the allied ground assault began, Baghdad radio announced that Saddam had ordered his troops to withdraw from Kuwait. Although White House spokesperson Marlin Fitzwater had stated a

Several thousand antiwar demonstrators rally in the streets of Seattle, Washington, on January 19, 1991. Although antiwar sentiment was strong and widespread in the United States and Europe during the war, demonstrations such as this one received little media attention.

Citizens show their support for the U.S. military action in the Persian Gulf at a rally in Montpelier, Vermont, on February 9, 1991. Such demonstrations were common across the United States as bombs rained over Baghdad and U.S. troops prepared for a ground assault on Iraqi troops in Kuwait.

few days earlier that "the United States and its coalition partners . . . will not attack retreating Iraqi forces," the allied bombing continued with full force, destroying convoys of trucks and cars as they fled Kuwait City. New York's *Newsday* quoted one Marine commander who described the whole affair as "a turkey shoot." Meanwhile, U.S. forces moved their heavy machinery across the desert. *Newsday* later reported that thousands of Iraqi soldiers who refused to surrender were deliberately buried alive in their trenches as U.S. tanks and earthmovers advanced over a 70-mile stretch along the Saudi border. Schwarzkopf's staff estimated that from air and ground attacks between 50,000 and 75,000 Iraqis were killed in their trenches. By most accounts, Iraqi resistance, even from the so-called elite Iraqi Republican Guard, was minimal.

The ground war ended just four days after it had begun. Contrary to expectations, Saddam had not used chemical weapons, and the allied forces had suffered fewer than 200 casualties. In Israel, four people were killed by Iraqi scud missiles, but even before this, on the second day of the war, Israel had gone on full nuclear alert and came within a hair's breadth of launching nuclear warheads.

The estimates of Iraqi dead, however, were, in Schwarzkopf's own words, "fifty, a hundred, a hundred and fifty thousand, perhaps more." In May, a Harvard University medical study team reported that as many as 170,000 deaths among children under 5 due to malnutrition and infectious diseases could occur in the aftermath of the war. The Iraqi government gave no casualty figures.

In the war's aftermath, the Palestinians were expelled from every country on the Gulf as punishment for supporting Saddam during the war. In the occupied territories, while Soviet Jews continued to arrive and settle, the Palestinians, who had been placed under a curfew during the six weeks of the offensive, emerged at the end of the war to find greatly expanded Jewish settlements. Many of them had

lost their jobs to the hundreds of thousands of newly arrived Soviet Jews.

Meanwhile, Kuwaiti oil wells burned out of control,
spewing noxious fumes and odors over the entire Gulf
region. Iraqi soldiers had uncapped the Kuwaiti oil wells
and lighted them before leaving Kuwait as Saddam had
said they would. Besides providing a dense smoke cover for
Iraqi troops, this was a retaliatory measure. After the war,
the smoke continued to billow over southern Kuwait, block-
ing out the sunlight for months. Environmentalists calculated that the damage worldwide to the environment and the
climate in the region might be permanent. Thanks to the
efforts of an international team of fire fighters, including
brigades from Iran and Eastern Europe, the wells would end
up taking only some nine months to recap.

When it was all over, everything Saddam had worked
to build in Iraq since he had joined the Baath party as a
young man, more than 30 years before, had been destroyed
before his eyes. Iraq's schools and hospitals, its agricultural
development, and its transportation and telecommunica-

*Former U.S. attorney
general Ramsey Clark
visited Iraq in early
February 1991 and re-
turned with film footage of
the devastation caused by
U.S. air strikes. He told of
widespread damage to the
civilian infrastructure, but
the U.S. news media mostly
ignored the story.*

U.S. marines capture a surrendering Iraqi soldier on February 25, 1991. Having spent months in desert trenches with limited food and water, the Iraqi troops put up little resistance as the U.S.-led coalition moved into Kuwait, and the ground war lasted only four days.

tions systems were in shambles. His army and his country lay in ruin. A UN inspection team estimated that some 9,000 civilian homes had been bombed, leaving at least 70,000 Iraqis homeless. Saddam reportedly offered to resign but was told by senior members of the party and the army that he got them into trouble and that it was up to him to get them out. There was a fear that Iraq could disintegrate.

Clearly, getting Iraq out of trouble would not be easy. Immediately after the U.S.-Iraqi cease-fire was signed, a civil war began (with heavy Iranian and U.S. encouragement) in northern and southern Iraq. In the south, armed Shiites rose up against Saddam, while the Kurds revolted in the north and briefly took control of the area. The Iraqi army put down one bloody revolt after another and began to take back the Iraqi cities from the rebel groups. Millions of Kurds fled to the north fearing reprisals from Saddam and set up camp in the mountains, where they soon began to freeze and starve to death.

The international news media focused on the terrible suffering in the Kurdish refugee camps. Iraqis throughout the rest of the country, who were also suffering tremendous hardship in the aftermath of the war, wondered why the Kurds had been singled out as the only Iraqis worthy of international compassion. Massoud Barzani, the Kurd-

ish guerrilla leader, went to Israel to try to get support for the uprising but failed because Israel believed that if the Kurds achieved independence it would set a bad precedent for the Palestinians. This time, Israel agreed to send only humanitarian aid.

In the United States, the plight of the Kurds was portrayed as evidence that Saddam's evil was still at work, and many Americans called for the U.S. military to "finish the job" and oust the Iraqi leader. While each night the evening news showed gruesome images from 1988 of gassed Kurds lying dead in the streets of Halabja, some Democrats in Congress who had voted for continued sanctions instead of war began to criticize the Bush administration for not having imposed democracy on Iraq the way the United States had done in Germany and Japan at the end of World War II. They said it had been a mistake to call off the military offensive without going all the way to Baghdad and capturing Saddam.

A Kurdish woman comforts her child. Believing Saddam's regime was weakened by the war and distracted by revolts in the south, the Kurds rebelled in the north. But as Iraqi forces moved in to reclaim the land, millions of Kurds fled for the mountains and set up refugee camps such as this one.

Others pointed out that the UN mandate was limited to freeing Kuwait.

At the end of March, the United States sent troops into northern Iraq to make it safe for the Kurds to return home. In April, the Kurdish leaders began negotiating an autonomy agreement with Saddam, based on his 1970 proposal. Many months later, it had not been concluded.

After the Gulf war, Saddam was no longer popular in Iraq. Even many of his followers now pointed to his failure to win the chess game with George Bush and blamed him for the devastation that had resulted. The accomplishments for which Saddam had been lauded in the past were forgotten. But, because under Saddam the Baathis had never allowed any opposition leadership to develop, either within or outside the party, there was no one to take Saddam's place.

Although Saddam announced that the process of democratization, interrupted by the Gulf crisis, would begin again, in order to move toward a constitution and a multiparty system with elections, most people put little faith in a man who had brought them such failure on the battlefield. Moreover, people were too busy trying to survive to think much about democracy. Iraqis now spent each day going from market to market looking for affordable food, even baking their own bread to cut costs. Contrary to what Bush had hoped, most of them, especially in the cities (where nearly half the population resided) were not ready to make a revolution.

Nevertheless, Shiite and Kurdish rebellions continued throughout the country, and crime rose sharply. Already a police state when the Baathis came to power in 1968— what with the Kurdish rebellions, the Iraqi Communist plots, and the interference at one time or another by both superpowers and by all of Iraq's neighbors except Jordan—Iraq's oppressive state security measures had never ceased, despite Saddam's progress on many other fronts. Now, faced with the possibility of a pro-Iran Shiite religious party victory at the polls, Saddam dropped all plans for democratization in favor of increasing military and police action to restore order.

Meanwhile, Bush vowed that until Saddam was gone he would veto any attempt to lift the UN sanctions against Iraq, making it impossible for the Iraqis to begin to rebuild in any meaningful way. The repairs to the bridges, the factories, the power grid, the telecommunications system, were only temporary. Unless spare parts could be imported, everything would collapse again in a few months. Moreover, the Iraqi government claimed to have almost no money for medicines and food because Iraq's assets, including all its foreign currency reserves, remained frozen abroad. It was estimated by the Arab-American Medical Association in the summer that as a result some 500 children a day were dying of malnutrition. The sanctions were proving even more far-reaching and devastating than the military offensive itself.

Although Iraq had agreed to comply with all the measures imposed by the cease-fire, Saddam and Bush continued to be at odds into late 1991. In September, after a UN inspection team charged with destroying all Iraqi weapons of mass destruction reported discovering several nuclear weapons facilities in Iraq, Bush put U.S. forces on alert, raising the prospect that the United States might once again use military force against Iraq.

On the anniversary of the war in January 1992, the White House announced a continuation of the sanctions against Iraq, and it was revealed that the United States was considering arming the Shiites and the Kurds and also sending the U.S. Air Force to provide them with air cover. Meanwhile, the Iraqi people continued to struggle under the tremendous burden imposed by the UN sanctions, and Saddam, for whom the war was not over, prepared for a long siege. One day when the war was over, he would make plans for his country's future. It was not the first time, after all, that Iraq had been destroyed, only to rebuild.

Further Reading

Arkin, William M., Damian Durrant, and Marianne Cherni. *On Impact: Modern Warfare and the Environment, A Case Study of the Gulf War.* Washington, DC: Greenpeace, May 1991.

Bani-Sadr, Abol Hassan. *My Turn to Speak*: *Iran, the Revolution & Secret Deals with the U.S.* New York: The Free Press, 1991.

Batatu, Hanna. *The Old Social Classes and the Revolutionary Movements of Iraq: A Study of Iraq's Old Landed and Commercial Classes and of Its Communists, Ba'thists and Free Officers.* Princeton, NJ: Princeton University Press, 1979.

Cockburn, Andrew, and Leslie Cockburn. *Dangerous Liaison: The Inside Story of the U.S.-Israeli Covert Relationship.* New York: HarperCollins, 1991.

Draper, Theodore. *A Very Thin Line: The Iran-Contra Affair.* New York: Hill & Wang, 1991.

Fernea, Elizabeth W. *Guests of the Sheik: An Ethnology of an Iraqi Village.* New York: Doubleday, 1969.

Helms, Christine M. *Iraq: The Eastern Flank of the Arab World.* Washington, DC: Brookings Institution, 1984.

Henderson, Simon. *Instant Empire: Saddam Hussein's Ambition for Iraq.* San Francisco: Mercury House, 1991.

Hersh, Seymour M. *The Samson Option: Israel's Nuclear Arsenal and American Foreign Policy.* New York: Random House, 1991.

Hirst, David. *The Gun and the Olive Branch: The Roots of Violence in the Middle East.* Winchester, MA: Faber and Faber, 1984.

Hitti, Philip K. *The Arabs: A Short History.* Washington, DC: Gateway Editions, 1990.

Iskander, Amir. *Saddam Hussein: The Fighter, the Thinker, and the Man.* Paris: Hachette Réalités, 1980.

Lawrence, T. E. *Seven Pillars of Wisdom.* New York: Penguin Books, 1976.

Marr, Phebe. *The Modern History of Iraq.* Boulder, CO: Westview Press, 1985.

Matar, Fuad. *Saddam Hussein: The Man, the Cause and the Future.* London, England: Third World Center, 1981.

Miller, Judith, and Laurie Mylroie. *Saddam Hussein and the Crisis in the Gulf.* New York: Times Books, 1991.

Ostrovsky, Victor, and Claire Hoy. *By Way of Deception: The Making and Unmaking of a Mossad Officer.* New York: St. Martin's Press, 1990.

Pachachi, Adnan. *Iraq's Voice at the UN: 1959–69.* London: Quartet Books, 1991.

Pelletier, Stephen C., Douglas Johnson, and Leif Rosenberger. *Iraq, Power and US Security in the Middle East.* Carlisle Barracks, PA, Strategic Studies Institute, US Army War College: US Government Printing Office, 1990.

Ridgeway, James. *The March to War.* New York: Four Walls Eight Windows, 1991.

Roux, Georges. *Ancient Iraq.* New York: Penguin Books, 1976.

Salibi, Kamal S. *History of Arabia.* Delmar, NY: Caravan Books, 1980.

Salinger, Pierre, and Eric Laurent. *Secret Dossier: The Hidden Agenda Behind the Gulf War.* New York: Penguin Books, 1991.

Sick, Gary. *October Surprise: America's Hostages in Iran and the Election of Ronald Reagan.* New York: Times Books/Random House, 1991.

Sifry, Micah L., and Christopher Cerf, eds. *The Gulf War Reader: History, Documents, Opinions.* New York: Times Books/Random House, 1991.

U.S. News & World Report. *Triumph Without Victory: The Unreported History of the Persian Gulf War.* New York: Times Books/Random House, 1992.

Woodward, Bob. *The Commanders.* New York: Simon & Schuster, 1991.

Chronology

April 28, 1937	Saddam Hussein is born in Tikrit
1947	Baath party founded in Syria
1948	The state of Israel proclaimed in Palestine; Arabs defeated in the first Arab-Israeli war
1956	Egyptian president Gamal Nasser nationalizes the Suez Canal on July 27; Saddam joins the Iraqi Baath party; Israeli Army invades Sinai on October 27; cease-fire called on November 6
1958	The British-supported monarchy in Iraq is ousted by General Abdul Karim Kassem, who declares a republic; Egypt and Syria form the United Arab Republic
1959	Saddam is charged with killing a government official but is released after the charges are dropped; takes part in unsuccessful plot to assassinate Kassem; flees to Syria
1960	Enrolls in Cairo University Law School
1961	Britain announces Kuwait's independence; Iraq refuses to recognize Kuwait's independence and threatens to invade; Britain, backed by a coalition that includes the United States, Egypt, Syria, and Saudi Arabia, sends troops to Kuwait
February 1963	The Baath party carries out a coup in Iraq; Saddam is appointed chief of Central Peasants Bureau
November 1963	The Baathis are ousted by the military; Saddam appointed head of the paramilitary arm of the party and plans a coup for the following year
1964	Saddam is jailed for political activity; elected a member of the Baath party National Command while in prison
1966	Escapes from prison; elected deputy secretary general of the Iraqi Baath party
1967	Arabs defeated in the Six-Day War; Israel occupies part of Egypt, Jordan, and Syria

1968	Baathis regain power; Saddam becomes Iraq's vice-president
1973	Syria and Egypt attack Israel; Egypt achieves partial victory
1975	Saddam and the shah of Iran sign the Algiers Accord
1978	Saddam hosts the Baghdad Summit of Arab leaders to repudiate the Camp David accords; diplomatic ties with Egypt are broken, and Egypt is expelled from the Arab League
1979	Saddam becomes president of Iraq; attends a summit of the Nonaligned Movement in Havana, Cuba
February 1980	Saddam proposes the Arab National Charter
September 4, 1980	Iran, under the Ayatollah Khomeini, shells several Iraqi border towns and oil refineries and closes the Shatt Al-Arab, Iraq's only outlet to the sea
September 22, 1980	Iraq retaliates against Iran; Israel begins selling U.S. weapons and spare parts to Iran despite a U.S. embargo of military sales to Iran
1981	Israel bombs Iraq's nuclear reactors
November 1984	Iraq and the United States restore diplomatic relations, broken after the 1967 war
1986	Iran-contra scandal breaks, and U.S.-Iraqi relations cool
1988	Iran-Iraq war ends; Kuwait begins its economic war on Iraq by driving down the price of oil
1990	In July, Saddam deploys troops on Kuwait's border; in August, Iraq invades Kuwait and U.S. troops land in Saudi Arabia
1991	U.S.-led coalition attacks Iraq by air on January 17; ground war begins on February 24; cease-fire declared four days later; Saddam remains in power and begins to rebuild Iraq

Index

PICTURE CREDITS

Nita M. Renfrew is a freelance journalist specializing in U.S. intelligence and national security affairs whose articles have appeared in *New York Magazine*, *The Wall Street Journal*, and *Foreign Policy*. A consultant to ABC News and the television program "Frontline," she has visited Iraq and the Middle East numerous times and was a frequent commentator on both radio and television during the Persian Gulf war.

Vito Perrone is Director of Teacher Education and Chair of Teaching, Curriculum, and Learning Environments at Harvard University. He has previous experience as a public school teacher, a university professor of history, education, and peace studies (University of North Dakota), and as dean of the New School and the Center for Teaching and Learning (both at the University of North Dakota). Dr. Perrone has written extensively about such issues as educational equity, humanities curriculum, progressive education, and evaluation. His most recent books are: *A Letter to Teachers: Reflections on Schooling and the Art of Teaching*; *Enlarging Student Assessment in Schools*; *Working Papers: Reflections on Teachers, Schools, and Communities*; *Visions of Peace*; and *Johanna Knudsen Miller: A Pioneer Teacher.*